The Beaver Book of the Air

Here is the ideal book for all flight enthusiasts who want to learn more about their subject. It tells the thrilling story of man's conquest of the air – from the basic principles of flight to supersonic jets and rockets – including the pioneering days, record achievements, air races like the Schneider Trophy, plus modern airliners, military aircraft and even flying cowboys! There is also a useful glossary of people, from John Alcock to Ferdinand von Zeppelin, to remind you who did what, and when.

J. D. Storer is Keeper in the Department of Technology at the Royal Scottish Museum, and he also runs an aircraft museum on the East Fortune airfield near Edinburgh. He has written several books about flying and aircraft, including another Beaver paperback, *Flying Feats*.

The Beaver Book of the AIR

J. D. Storer

Illustrated by John Batchelor and Peter Dennis

Beaver Books

First published in 1979 by
The Hamlyn Publishing Group Limited
London · New York · Sydney · Toronto
Astronaut House, Feltham, Middlesex, England

ISBN 0 600 30387 x

Set, printed and bound in England by
Cox & Wyman Ltd.,
London, Reading and Fakenham
Set in Monotype Old Style

Contents

1 The Air

Air – what is it?

Without air, aviation as we know it today would not be possible because all aircraft are truly craft of the air. Balloons and airships float in air for they are *lighter-than-air* craft. Aeroplanes rely upon wings moving through the air to lift them off the ground. The early aviators often referred to the wings as *planes* hence the name *aeroplane* (or *airplane* in America) and the use of *monoplane* for an aeroplane with one wing or *biplane* for two wings. In addition to using air to provide lift, most aircraft have engines which need the oxygen in air to burn their fuel and so produce power.

Air is a mixture of gases made up of one-fifth oxygen, nearly four-fifths nitrogen and very small quantities of several other gases. Of all these, oxygen is the most important because living creatures need to breathe oxygen in order to survive. When the American astronauts landed on the surface of the moon they

The family tree

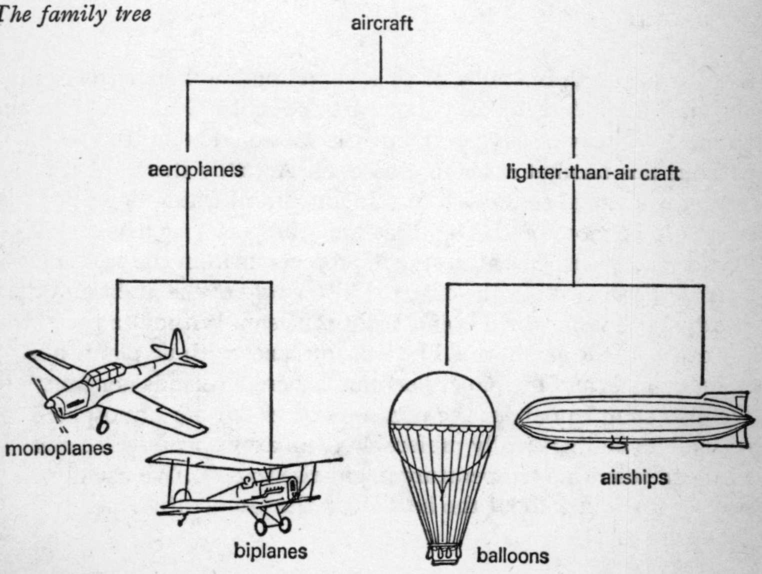

carried their own supply of oxygen because there is no air on the moon. On earth oxygen plays another very important part in our lives because it is essential if a fire is to burn, and life would be very difficult without fire in one form or another. Not only do we burn fuel to keep warm and to cook, but also fuel is burned in motor car engines and many other sources of power.

Early scientists found it very difficult to understand and explain the relationship between air and fire. In fact they got the story wrong and it was not corrected until the eighteenth century. Several scientists helped to discover the gases which make up our air and one of the best known was an English clergyman called Joseph Priestley. In 1774 Priestley discovered oxygen, which he called dephlogisticated air, and announced his discovery to the world. For the Swedish chemist, Karl Scheele, this announcement came as an unpleasant surprise, for Scheele had already discovered oxygen, but as he had not published his findings Priestley received the honours. All too often discoveries and inventions are confused by claims and counter claims. Incidentally, Priestley also discovered nitrogen.

Atmosphere

Around the earth is a layer of air several hundred kilometres high and this *atmosphere* makes life on earth possible. Even if we had an unlimited supply of oxygen to breathe we would be in trouble without this blanket of air to protect us. Actually the blanket is not pure air for it contains a certain amount of water, or *water vapour* to be more precise, and several other gases such as *carbon dioxide* and *ozone*. Our atmosphere protects us from the scorching heat of the sun during the day, the bitter cold of the night and the harmful radiation which is emitted by the sun. Without a protecting atmosphere, the earth would be a dead planet with no plants and trees, animals and birds, neither would there be clouds nor rain. We may complain about the rain sometimes but our atmosphere with all its faults is really preferable to an atmosphere-less earth where the daytime temperature might rise to 80°C. We usually start complaining about the heat when the temperature rises above 25–30°C!

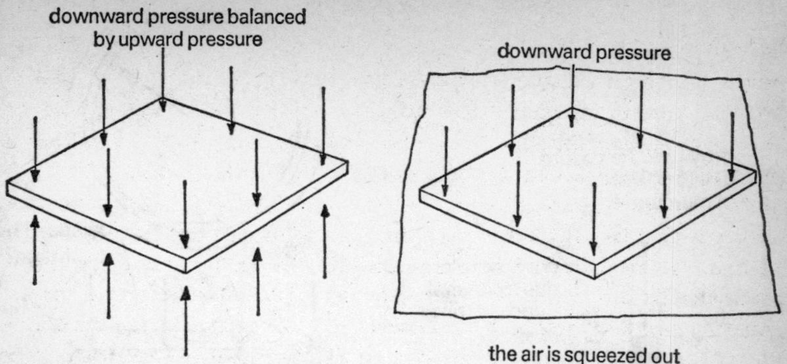

Air pressure demonstrated

Air pressure and density

We think of air as being light: in fact the expression 'as light as air' is often used, but air does have weight. A cube of air with sides of just 1 metre would weigh over 1 kilogram. So the *density* of air at sea level is about 1.23 kilograms per cubic metre. Now every square metre of the earth's surface supports a column of air several hundred kilometres high and weighing some 10,000 kilograms yet, if we hold out a thin sheet of wood 1 metre square we are not aware of this great load. Although we are being subjected to an air *pressure* of 10,000 kilograms per square metre we do not feel it because pressure in a liquid, or gas, is equal in all directions. In other words the downward pressure on the upper surface of the wood is balanced by an upward pressure on the lower surface. All we feel is the weight of the piece of wood. Air pressure can be demonstrated by taking two flat surfaces, glass being better than wood, and eliminating the air between them. This is easily done by wetting the surfaces in contact and pressing them gently together. It is almost impossible to separate the faces except by sliding them apart in which case the air returns to all sides. This is the principle of the rubber 'sucker'.

Atmospheric pressure is measured by the familiar barometer which compares the column of air from ground level to outer space, against a more manageable column of mercury giving the same pressure. A normal reading at sea level would be 760 mm or 30 inches and any variation up or down would indicate good or bad

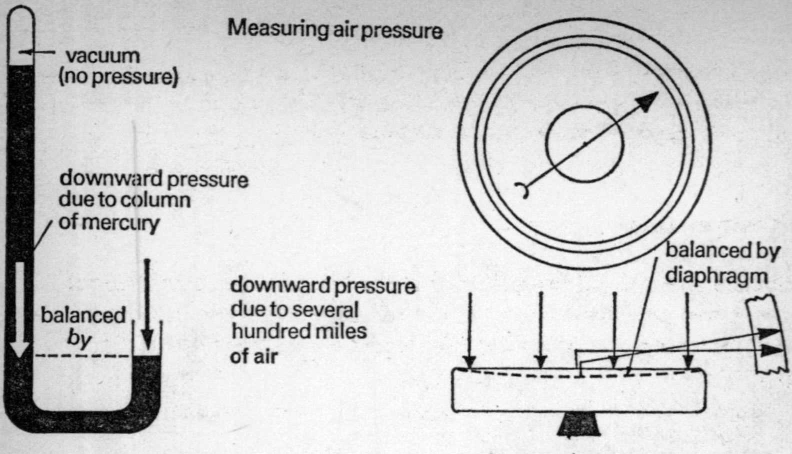

Measuring air pressure

A mercury barometer

An aneroid barometer

weather. But the atmospheric pressure would also drop if we moved upwards. The higher we go, the less air there is above us, so the weight of this column of air has been reduced. If a barometer is taken up in an aircraft the pressure will drop as the aircraft climbs. Now if we know the pressure at each altitude we can use the barometer to determine our altitude. This is the principle of the simple altimeter which is carried by all aircraft.

If you have ever climbed a high mountain you may have found yourself unusually short of breath on the higher slopes. This is due to the air becoming thinner at higher altitudes. By 'thin air' we mean that there is less air in a cubic metre, or in other words, the density has decreased. For example, a cubic metre of air at sea level weighs about 1 kilogram, but at the summit of Mount Everest this same volume would weigh less than 0.5 kilogram – less than half the density at sea level.

Less air means less oxygen and this explains why mountaineers at very high altitudes become exhausted after only two or three steps. To overcome this problem the conquerors of Everest carried their own supply of oxygen in lightweight cylinders strapped to their backs. Oxygen has been carried by high-flying military aircraft for many years but an oxygen mask, covering nose and mouth, would not be very acceptable to an airline passenger. An alternative solution was found by which the thin air was compressed by air compressors and pumped into the aircraft's cabin. This increased the pressure inside the cabin and brought the density back to a more comfortable level. *Pressurised* aircraft were first used during the early days of the Second World War and some ten years later their numbers increased rapidly as the high flying jet and turbo-prop airliners entered service.

Air temperature

Like the density and pressure of air, the temperature also changes as we travel upwards. However the temperature does not drop steadily, instead, it fluctuates. The upper atmosphere has been

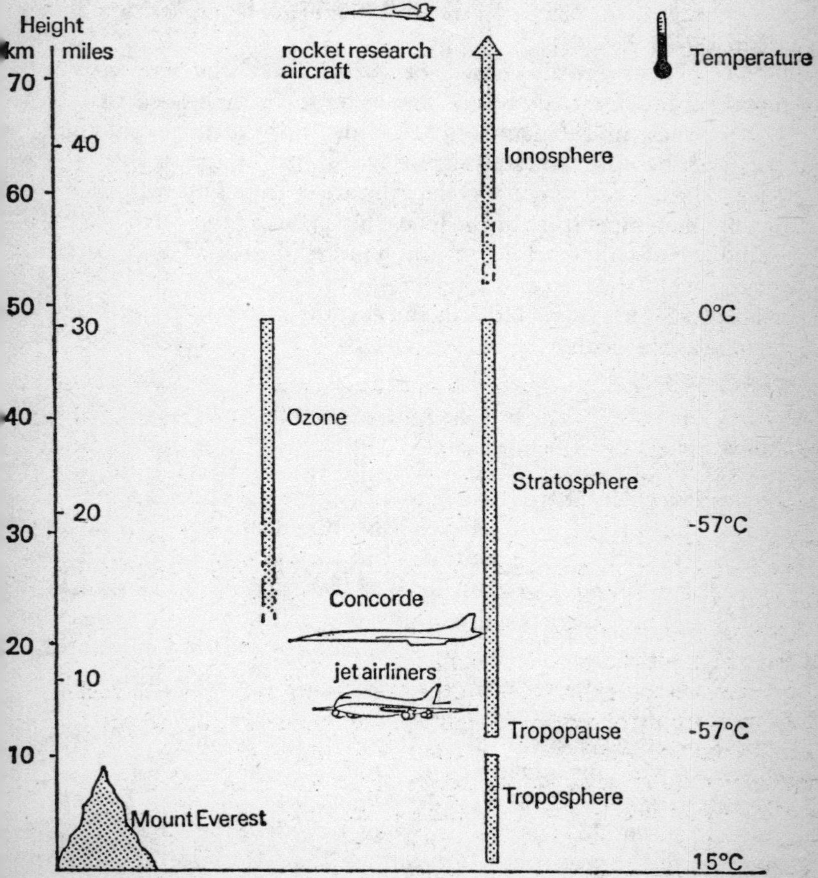

divided into invisible layers and the temperature pattern varies in each layer. The first is known as the *troposphere* and this extends from sea level to a height of some 11 kilometres. The temperature drops steadily from 15°C at sea level to −57°C at the upper boundary of the troposphere called the *tropopause*. Above the troposphere comes 40 kilometres of *stratosphere* where for a while the temperature stays at about −57°C. This is the realm of present day long-range jet airliners. At 30 to 50 km up we find a layer rich in ozone which absorbs some of the rays from the sun giving a sort of twilight and a rise in temperature to 0°C. Another drop in temperature takes place and we enter the black *ionosphere* at about 60 km above the earth.

The ionosphere really consists of several layers which are very important because radio waves bounce off them back to earth. Without these invisible mirrors long-range transmitting would be impossible because the radio signals would just disappear into space. Signals of different wavelengths are reflected by various layers. The temperature in the ionosphere rises as the earth is left behind, eventually reaching several hundred degrees. The ionosphere is the home of auroras and is the graveyard of most of the meteorites which travel towards the earth from outer space. They burn up as they enter the outer regions of the earth's protecting atmosphere.

Winds

Our restless atmosphere is made up of huge masses of air, some warmer than others, pushing each other about the sky. In area they may be as large as a continent but they stretch far up into the atmosphere too. The boundaries of these aerial continents are called *fronts* and these usually bring cloud and rain (see Weather forecasting, page 16). Within these boundaries a further movement takes place as air moves around a region of low or high pressure so producing winds.

Back in the days of the sailing ship, captains would go well out of their way to take advantage of favourable winds and direct routes were ignored if they involved fighting a head wind. In some parts of the world the prevailing winds remain in the same direction all the year round, for example Cape Horn at the southern tip of South America very rarely has anything but a strong westerly wind. By contrast some tropical countries are subjected to heavy summer rains or monsoons and in these areas the prevailing winds reverse completely between winter and summer.

The ordinary surface winds do not affect modern airliners very seriously although extra fuel may have to be carried to combat a strong head wind. At an altitude of some 13 kilometres, however, a super-wind, called the *jet-stream,* is to be found in certain parts of the world. It was first encountered by high altitude bombers flying to Japan towards the end of the Second World War. The crews reported meeting steady westerly winds of 400 km/h (248 mph) and occasionally speeds of up to 600 km/h (373 mph) were encountered. Head winds like this resulted in the aircraft actually flying backwards and made the average hurricane of 150 km/h (93 mph) seem like a gentle breeze. For many years this new discovery was investigated but progress was slow because an invisible stream of air constantly changing its path was not an easy thing to track down. As information gradually became available the pattern of the jet-stream became clearer until today it is as predictable as any wind. Airliners 'hitch-hike' when it happens to be going their way but otherwise they are careful to avoid it.

Gusts and turbulence

An aeroplane can be flying along quite steadily when suddenly it seems to drop and then recover. These bumps were originally called *air pockets* because to the people flying it felt as though the aircraft had fallen into a pocket, but we now know that they are caused by the aircraft flying through a gust. A gust is a column of air moving up, down or sideways. An up-gust of hot air or *thermal* is the most widely known because it is used by model enthusiasts and glider pilots to lift their machines skywards (see Kites and gliders, page 30). Hot air is lighter than cold air and so it rises upwards, taking with it any light aircraft.

Smaller bumps are due to turbulent air which is often encountered when flying through clouds – especially thunder clouds. In these conditions a pilot usually warns his passengers to fasten their seat belts. But in recent years pilots of high-flying jets have

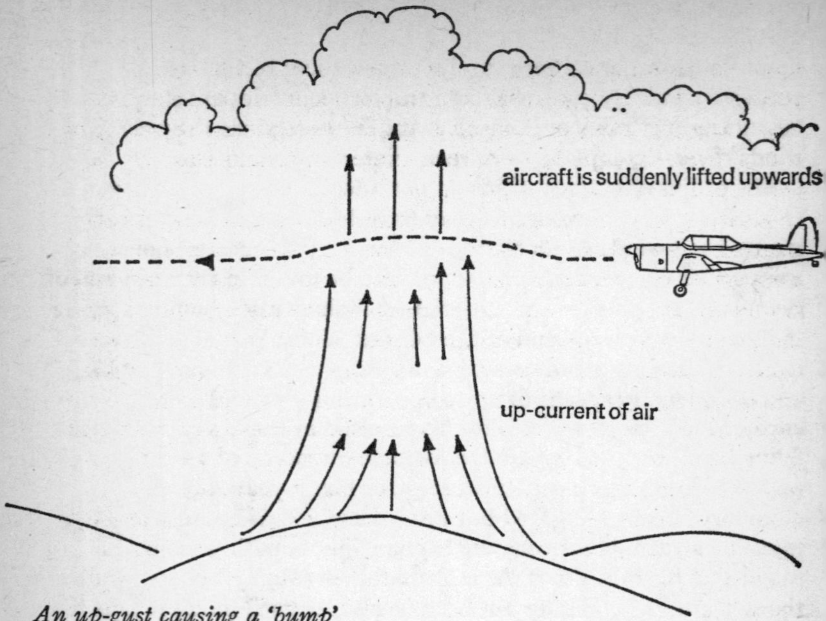

An up-gust causing a 'bump'

discovered a new kind of turbulence which cannot be seen. This is called *clear air turbulence* and it usually occurs near the jet-stream high altitude wind (see Winds, page 14).

Apart from the unpleasantness of a bumpy flight these gusts and turbulence reduce the life of an airliner. Up- and down-gusts cause the wings to flex and unfortunately there is a limit to the amount of flexing a wing can stand. This is called the *fatigue life*. Central Africa is a region particularly prone to gusts, consequently the life of a wing is shorter there. To make sure that the wing is not overworked an instrument to measure gusts may be fitted to the airliner.

Weather forecasting

Weather conditions are vitally important to all pilots, but the study of *meteorology* is a complicated business because weather has a habit of changing without warning – as we all know. Now we are only interested in the weather at ground level, but anyone flying needs to know about the weather at all altitudes, so it becomes a three-dimensional problem. An hour or so before take-off, an airline Captain calls in at the Meteorological Office to collect the latest weather forecast for his route. He is supplied with details of clouds, rain, fog, wind, pressures, temperatures and any storms which may be brewing up.

Weather forecasts are compiled from information supplied by weather stations around the world. Some of these stations are situated in the wastes of the Arctic and others on ships anchored in mid-Atlantic. Weather observers can easily take readings near the surface but to investigate the upper atmosphere they use balloons. Small radio sets in these *Radio Sonde* balloons send back vital information about winds, temperatures, etc. Ships and aircraft help the forecasters too by sending in radio reports about the weather they are meeting along their routes. In recent times a new dimension has been introduced into weather forecasting: unmanned satellites can look down on the clouds and send back pictures covering vast areas of the earth's surface.

Visibility is important particularly at each end of a flight and this is affected by clouds, rain and fog. If conditions change during a flight the Captain is told by radio and he may, in extreme circumstances, have to divert his airliner to another airport.

From our barometer we know that a sudden drop in pressure portends 'wet and windy' weather, but the meteorologist goes a step further and produces a map of the weather. This may sound impossible when you consider how quickly the weather can change, but rain clouds do not disappear when it stops raining, they just move on. In other words, if a weather map is drawn on a piece of tracing paper and placed over an ordinary map, the tracing paper should be made to move slowly across the map. Of course the weather map itself changes slightly but the main changes in weather are due to this overall movement, a movement which enables the weather to be forecast.

On a map of the ground, places at the same height are joined by contour lines and these reveal details of hills and valleys. On a weather map, places of equal pressure are joined by lines called isobars, and these are used in a similar way to give a 'picture' of pressure variations. High pressure is a sign of good weather: conversely, low pressure spells trouble and when the isobars are close together high winds can be expected. The boundaries of

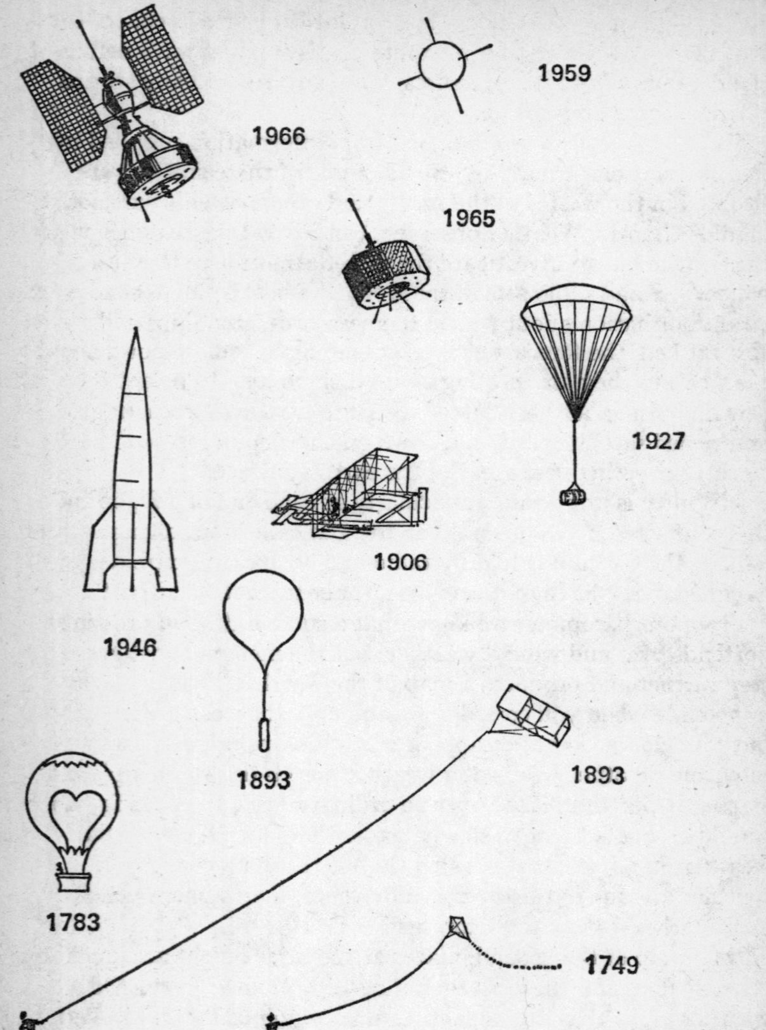

The evolution of devices for studying the atmosphere, resulting in today's satellites for weather forecasting.

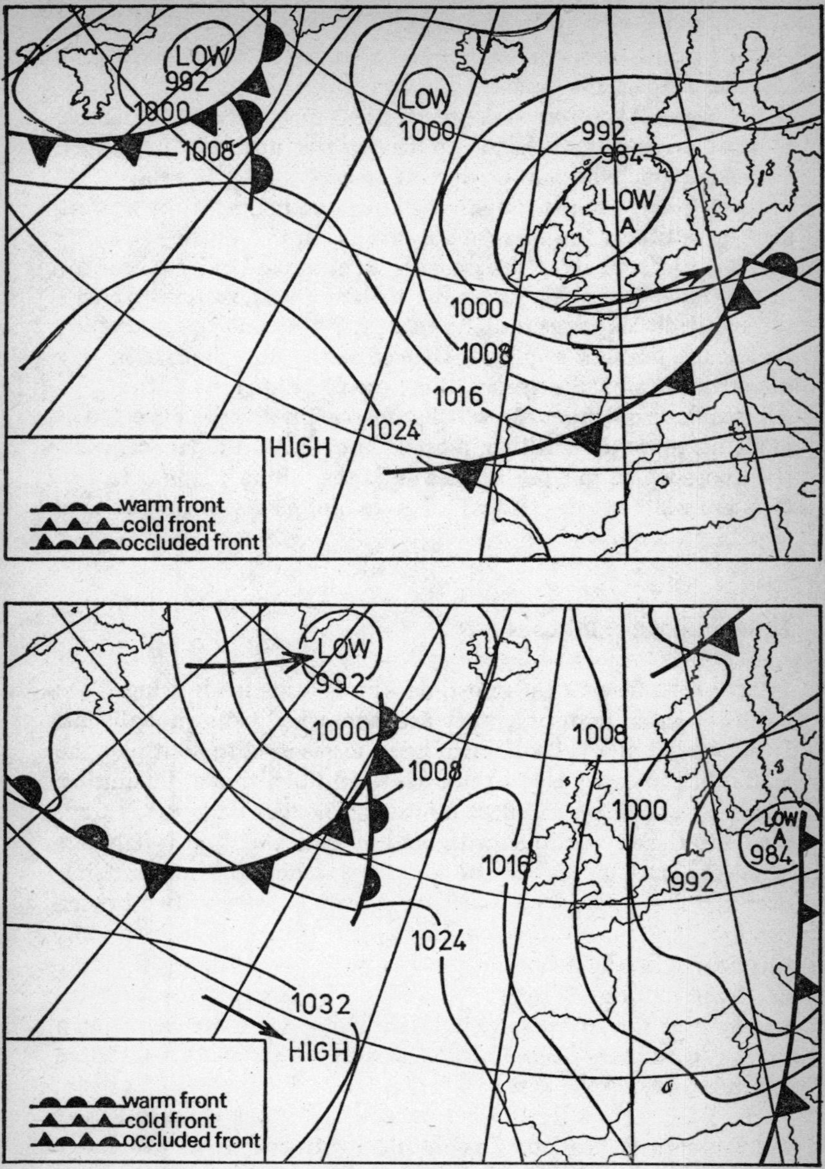

Weather maps for consecutive days showing movement of weather: Low A moves from northern Britain to Poland.

moving masses of warm or cold air called fronts are shown on the weather map by heavy lines.

We have all had some experience of storms. The most common mixture is a gale-force wind and driving rain but sometimes the ingredients include snow or thunder and lightning. If we are unlucky enough to get caught in a storm we make for the nearest shelter, but for an airliner caught in a storm there is no shelter and it is buffeted about. Passengers do not take kindly to this sort of treatment and neither does the structure of the aircraft. The buffeting strains wings, tailplanes, etc., far beyond their normal limits, and it might even cause one of them to break off with disastrous results. Storms are therefore to be avoided so the captain finds out from the weather forecast if any are expected along his route. In addition, most airliners have a radar scanner in their nose which can 'see' storms and other aircraft long before they are visible to the pilot. This gives him plenty of time to take avoiding action.

Lighter than air: balloons

In 1783 men flew for the first time – by floating in air using lighter-than-air craft or as they are more widely known, balloons. If the weight of a balloon, including the gas used to fill it plus the load it has to carry, is less than the weight of a similar volume of air then the balloon will float upwards. The first balloon to carry men into the air was filled with hot air because hot air is lighter than cold air. This fact can be seen by watching the hot air rising over any fire. This *hot air balloon* was built in 1783 by two French brothers, Joseph and Etienne Montgolfier, who did not wish to fly themselves, so the honour of the first aerial voyage went to Pilâtre de Rozier and the Marquis d'Arlandes. The Montgolfiers' balloon was open at the bottom and in this opening was a fire carried in a brazier. Gradually the balloon filled with hot air and lifted off the ground, carrying the first balloonists on a 9-kilometre flight over Paris. Two weeks later another balloon flight took place in France but this time the balloon was not filled with hot air. It was designed by Professor Jacques Charles, who was a scientist at the Paris Academy and therefore knew about the recently discovered gas –

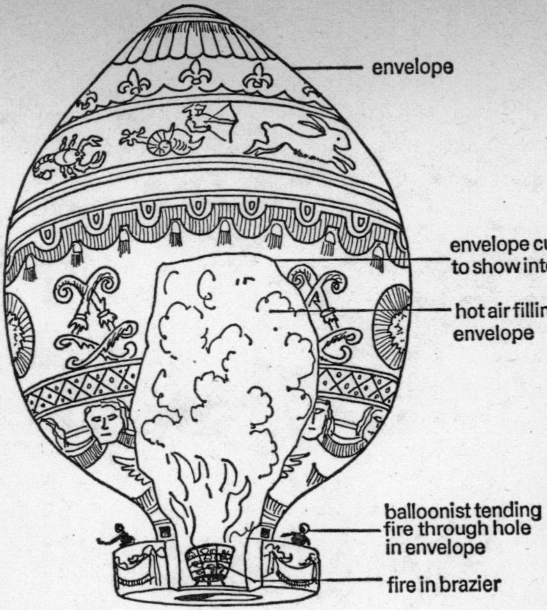

A Montgolfier hot air balloon

hydrogen. Now hydrogen is very much lighter than air, for example. A cubic metre of hydrogen weighs only 0.08 kilogram compared with 1.23 kilograms for a cubic metre of air. Professor Charles was assisted by two brothers, Ainé and Cadet Robert, and their balloon carried Charles and one of the brothers on a 43-kilometre (27-mile) cross-country flight.

Ballooning became a popular sport but as a means of transport these craft had one great disadvantage; they were at the mercy of the wind. A balloonist could only travel from A to B if the wind happened to be blowing in the direction A to B. Nevertheless, some remarkable balloon flights were made. In January 1785, a French balloonist called Jean-Pierre Blanchard and an American scientist Dr John Jeffries took off from Dover in a hydrogen balloon. The wind was blowing towards France but after a good start their balloon sank lower and lower. They threw everything they could spare overboard, even their clothes, and the balloon rose again. They reached France safely – but very cold! Several scientists followed Dr Jeffries' lead and explored the unknown atmosphere in balloons. The British pair, Coxwell and Glaisher, made many research flights and even tried to take aerial

Glaisher fainted at 29,000 feet while Coxwell opened a control valve with his teeth as his hands were numb with cold.

photographs. On one of their ascents during 1862 they reached a height of 7600 m (25,000 ft) – though this was more by accident than design, as a control valve stuck. Another series of balloon flights made history in 1870–71 when Paris was besieged by German troops. Many passengers and letters were carried by balloons from the city, over the surrounding troops, to safety – when the wind was blowing in the right direction of course.

Lighter than air: airships

Many attempts were made to control the direction of balloon flights, rather than letting them just drift with the wind. They were called *dirigible* (steerable) balloons or *airships*. Paddles and oars were tried but they had no effect and until a lightweight engine was invented there was little hope of success. Steam

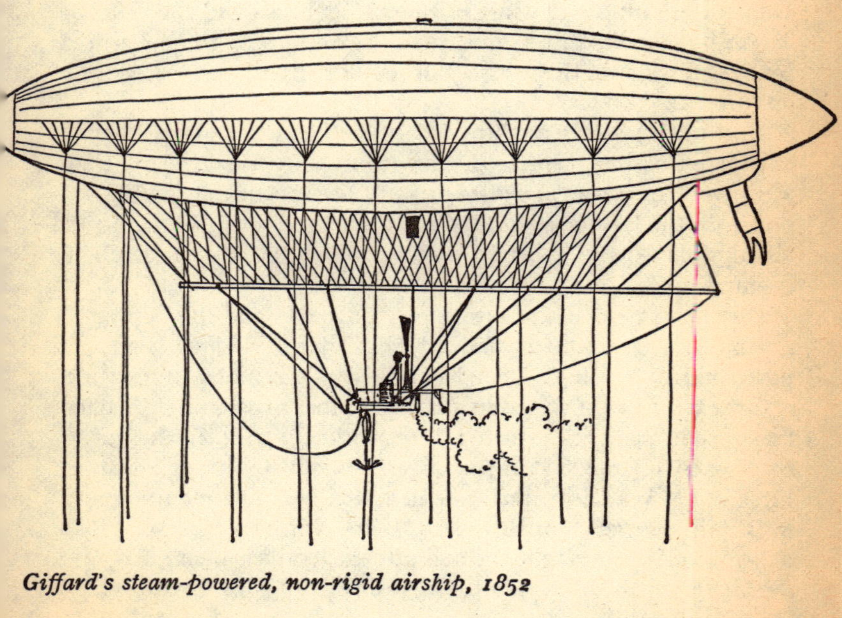

Giffard's steam-powered, non-rigid airship, 1852

Zeppelin rigid airship, 1914

engines, electric motors and petrol engines were fitted and eventually the petrol engine became the most successful. But even with the power of an engine, early airships still had trouble with strong headwinds. In 1901 the airship pioneer Alberto Santos-Dumont attempted to win a prize for a flight around the Eiffel Tower but several times he reached the tower only to be defeated by a head wind on the return journey. Eventually he succeeded and won 125,000 francs.

Most of these early airships consisted of a large sausage-shaped balloon with a *car* suspended below containing the crew and engine. They were known as *non-rigid* airships because of the flexible nature of the large gas bag. During the First World War non-rigid airships played an important part patrolling the seas in search of enemy ships.

Large non-rigid airships were very unwieldy and the German airship designer Count Ferdinand von Zeppelin designed huge and powerful *rigid* airships. They had a lightweight metal framework and the gas was contained in a large number of separate gas bags fixed inside the fabric-covered framework. By 1914 *Zeppelins* could carry a large load of passengers or bombs. Throughout the First World War Zeppelins were in action bombing many targets in Britain. However, airships filled with hydrogen were very dangerous if they caught fire and after several accidents, large airships were abandoned in the 1930s.

Wings: lift and drag

A balloon lifts into the air because it is lighter than air, but an aeroplane is heavier than air and must therefore find some other way of producing *lift*. The wing of an aeroplane moves quickly through the air and the flow of air over the wing produces an upwards force or lift. The study of air flowing around objects is called *aerodynamics* and one of the first aerodynamicists was the Ancient Greek philosopher Aristotle. He studied a projectile flying through the air and declared that in the wake of the projectile there was a region without air – in other words a *vacuum*. In this he was correct, but then his theory went astray for Aristotle suggested that the surrounding air rushing in to fill this vacuum pushed the projectile along. The opposite is in fact true, for this region of vacuum or *suction* behind the projectile tries to hold it back and thus slows it down. The air resistance at the nose of the projectile caused by a region of pressure also retards the projectile and the combined effect is known as *drag*. All high-speed vehicles suffer from the effects of drag and these include aeroplanes, cars, motor cycles and railway trains, but streamlining helps to reduce drag and so increase maximum speeds.

An aeroplane uses its wings to provide lift, which is unfortunately always accompanied by drag. This can be demonstrated by a simple experiment with a large sheet of cardboard. First hold the piece of cardboard at arm's length and on edge. Then turn around as fast as you can. You should be able to feel the air resistance or drag. Now repeat the experiment with the cardboard held flat and you will feel very little or no drag. To generate lift, twist your arm a little so that the higher edge of the cardboard is leading as you rotate. Then you should feel both lift and drag. You might also notice that the faster you move the cardboard wing, the more lift it produces – but with more drag. Likewise, if you increase the angle of slope, the lift – and drag – increase. You could also try a larger piece of cardboard and yet again both lift and drag would increase. This simple experiment has demonstrated some of the things which control lift and drag such as speed, angle of slope (or *incidence*) and wing area. Other factors which are more difficult to demonstrate are air density and wing shape. We have already discovered that the air at high altitudes is less dense – now this

1

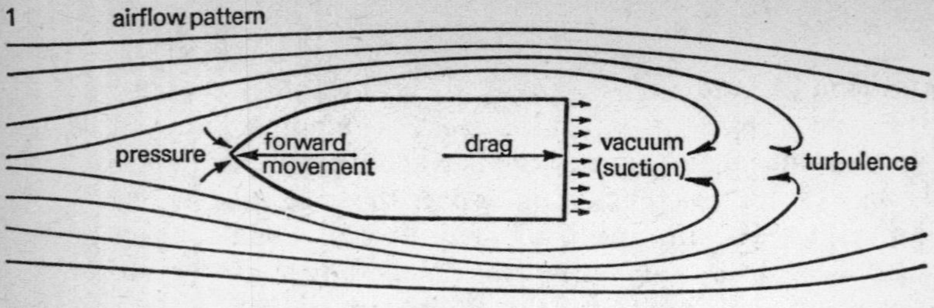

2

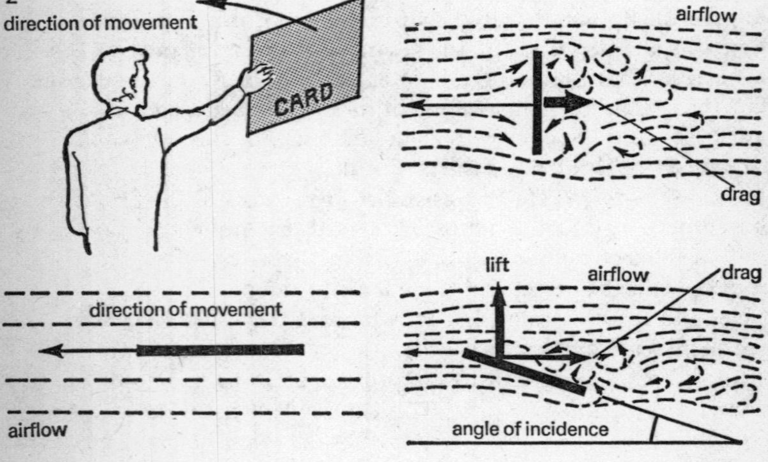

3

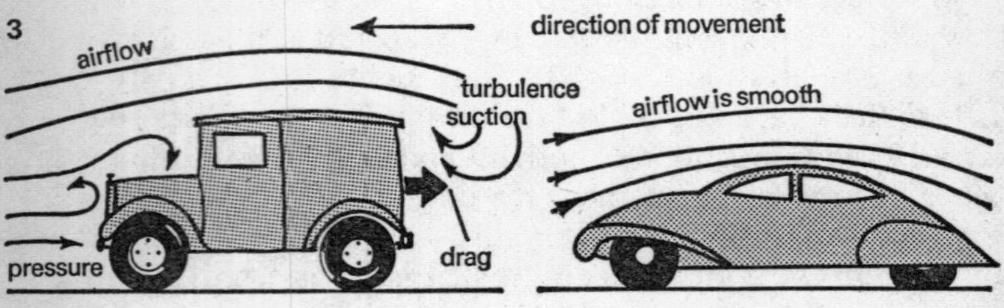

4

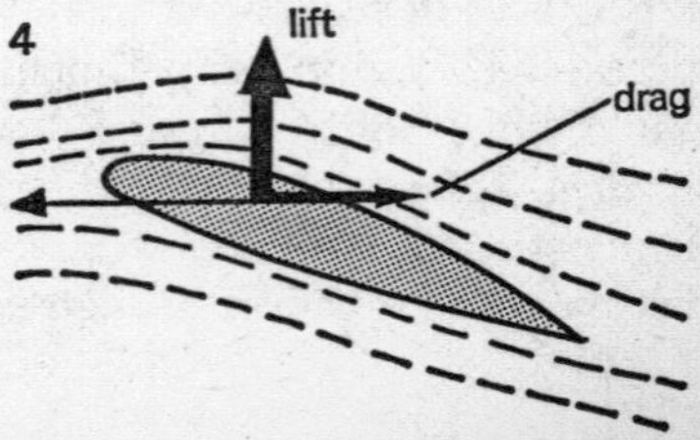

1 *Drag*
2 *Lift and drag demonstrated with piece of card*
3 *Drag reduced by streamlining*
4 *High lift: low drag with wing*

thinner air offers less resistance as one might expect, but it also provides less lift. By wing shape we mean the shape you would see if a wing were sliced vertically from front to rear. This shape includes the streamlining effect and is very important because a carefully designed shape is one of the few ways of increasing the lift without increasing the drag by the same amount. A good wing section produces pressure on the underside pushing it upwards, and suction on the upper surface also pulling it upwards. Surprisingly, the suction effect is the greater of the two upwards forces on a wing.

The experiment of holding a sheet of cardboard and spinning round is rather similar to the experiments carried out by the pioneer aerodynamicists. They used a machine called a *whirling arm* consisting of a mechanically driven arm which rotated. A model wing was fixed at the end of the arm and this was used to find out about the factors which control lift and drag.

Wind tunnels

In order to measure the lift and drag produced by a wing moving through air, early experimenters such as Sir George Cayley and Otto Lilienthal used a whirling arm. But they found it very difficult to take measurements of lift and drag on a wing which was rotating at high speed. There was a simple solution: keep the wing

A 'working section' of a simple wind tunnel

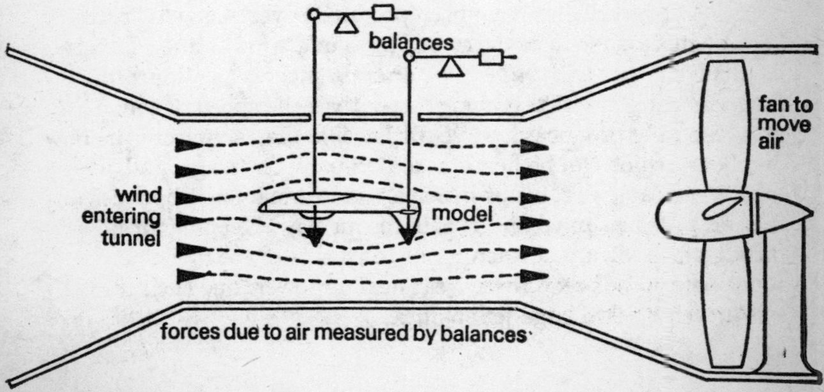

still and move the air. This was done in a *wind tunnel* which, as the name implies, was a tunnel through which air was blown by a powerful fan. A model wing, or even a complete aeroplane, was placed in the tunnel and supported on a balance or weighing machine. Then the air flow was turned on and the loads on the model under test could be measured. Wilbur and Orville Wright made almost 1000 flights with their final glider before they built the world's first powered aeroplane but they also carried out many other experiments. To assist with these experiments they built their own wind tunnel and Orville said it '. . . would enable us to calculate in advance the performance of a machine'. Well, today a wind tunnel is essential to do just that. Aircraft designers use a wind tunnel to test their ideas before risking them on the real thing. They find out about the overall shape of the new design and check many other details of the design such as the engine layout, the undercarriage and wheels, the streamlining and, of course, lift and drag. When the Vickers VC10 airliner was being designed, forty-four different wind tunnel models were constructed, each costing many thousands of pounds, and these models spent some 4000 hours under test. One important aspect ofthe wind tunnel tests is to study the flow of air around the new design and make sure that it flows smoothly – for turbulent air is a major source of drag. Of course air is invisible but it can be made visible by blowing smoke into the tunnel through tiny nozzles. The smoke emerges as lines and its path over the model can easily be seen. Another way of studying the flow of air is to stick tufts of wool or silk on to the surface of the model. Where the flow is smooth the tufts will lie down – all pointing in the same direction – but if there is any turbulence they will flutter.

As faster aeroplanes have been produced over the years it has become more difficult to carry out tests in a wind tunnel. This is particularly true with *supersonic* aircraft such as the Concorde. A supersonic aircraft travelling faster than the speed of sound unfortunately produces a wave, rather like the wave from the bow of a boat, which can be heard as a loud bang on the ground. This *sonic boom* causes problems inside a wind tunnel for it bounces off the walls of the tunnel and upsets the air flow. Keeping air flowing through a wind tunnel when it has to pass over the model at supersonic speeds requires a great deal of power: one such tunnel was driven by two large jet engines.

2 Flying Machines

Human birds: flapping wings

We do not know when man first tried to fly but it would be only natural for him to copy the birds One of the first flying stories came from Greek mythology. When Daedalus and his son Icarus were imprisoned on the island of Crete by King Minos, Daedalus refused to be beaten and made two sets of wings using feathers and wax. They escaped but young Icarus flew too high and the sun melted the wax holding his wings together so that he crashed into the sea and drowned. Of course this was only a story, but the idea of a flying machine based on bird flight, using flapping wings (and called an *ornithopter*) dominated the thoughts of early inventors. The great Leonardo da Vinci was no exception; he spent many hours studying and sketching the flight of birds. From these studies he produced several drawings of complicated ornithopters – which could never have worked – but he also sketched a model helicopter and a parachute which were quite practical.

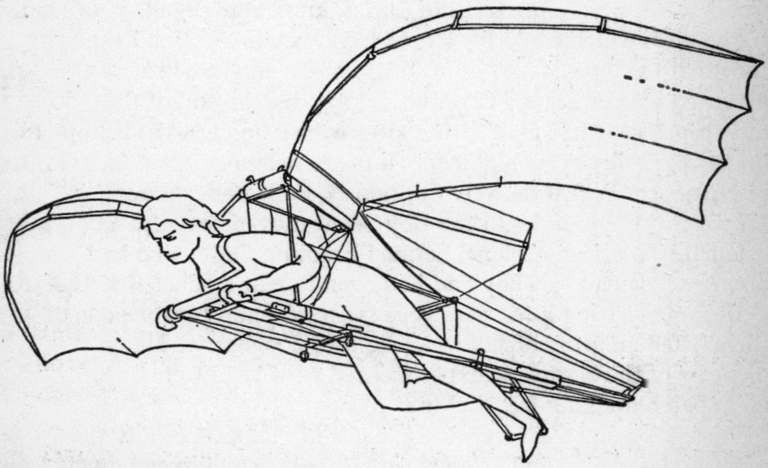

Leonardo da Vinci's ornithopter

Many hopeful 'tower-jumpers' tried their luck with flapping wings. One was an Italian called John Damian who made himself some wings of feathers and leaped from the wall of Stirling Castle. He crashed to the ground and escaped with a broken thigh. Damian blamed the feathers for his failure: he had used hens' feathers whereas he should have used the feathers of an eagle!

In 1680 an Italian scientist called Giovanni Borelli published a book which virtually ended the 'flapping-wing' idea. He put forward scientific reasons why human muscles were not strong enough to enable man to fly unaided. He also claimed that mechanical flapping wings were not a practical proposition. Borelli's predictions were very accurate for there has never been a really successful ornithopter and it took many years of experiments to produce a man-powered aeroplane which could make a short flight around a figure-of-eight course. In 1959 a prize of £5000 was offered for such a flight, but by 1973 it had not been claimed, so the prize was increased to £50,000: this was eventually won as recently as September 1977.

Kites and gliders

Kites have a very long history and appeared in many parts of the world. Even before the birth of Christ, kites were popular in China. Large kites which could lift a man were seen in the Far East by the great explorer Marco Polo. In Australia the box-kite was invented by Lawrence Hargrave in 1893. By the end of the nineteenth century, man-lifting kites were being used in Europe to lift military observers high enough to see behind enemy lines. Two kite pioneers in Britain were Captain B. F. S. Baden-Powell (brother of the founder of the Boy Scout movement) and a colourful American, Colonel Samuel Franklin Cody, who had previously been a cowboy and had even fought against Red Indians. Cody's man-lifting kites were very successful and by 1904 one of them lifted an army officer to a height of 400 metres. Many pioneers of the aeroplane experimented with kites to test their ideas before making free flights in *gliders*.

These pioneers also studied the flight of birds, especially the soaring flight of seagulls, hawks and eagles. They learned much about the shape of wings and how the birds controlled their flight,

Cody's man-lifting kite

Otto Lilienthal flying his hang-glider, which he controlled by swinging his legs about. Lilienthal built an artificial hill 15 metres high from which to launch his glider.

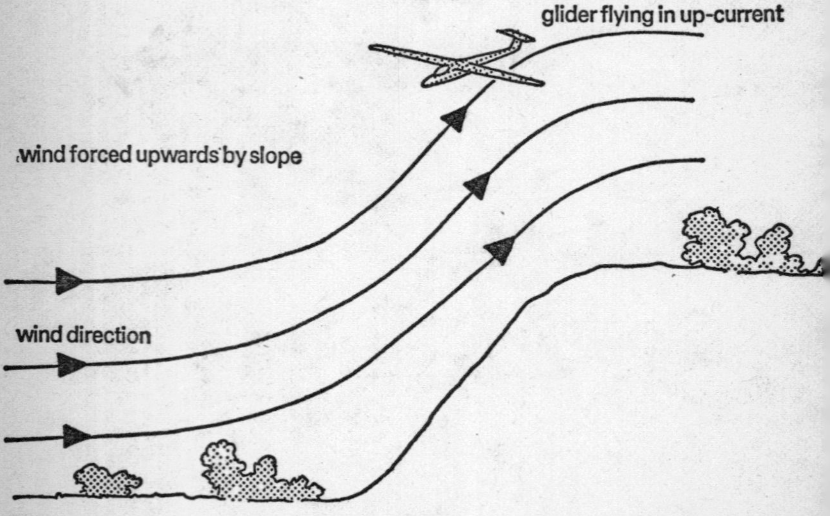

How a glider can fly using a slope: slope soaring

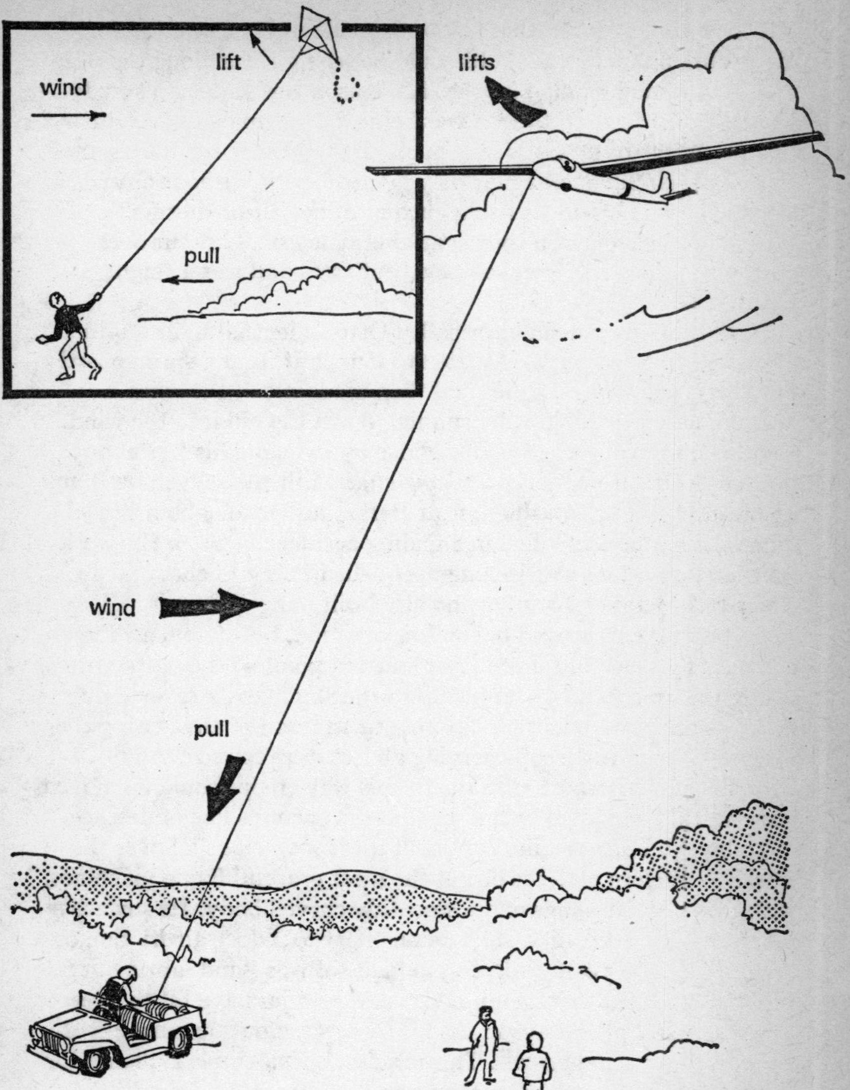

Launching a modern glider with a winch

but they also observed that the birds made use of any currents of air to obtain free lift. Seagulls could be seen gliding along the edge of a sea cliff and gaining height. The reason was simple: a steady wind blowing in from the sea was being forced up over the cliff and this produced an upwards flow of air. But inland birds were sometimes seen circling and again they gained height without any effort. They had found a rising current of hot air or thermal. When the sun shines on the earth, thermals usually occur over open land such as a ploughed field, but trees and water might produce down-gusts.

In 1891 a German engineer called Otto Lilienthal built a glider after studying the birds. He tried to launch it from a springboard but this did not work. Lilienthal then made use of the wind blowing up a gentle slope by running down the hill into the wind. Once airborne he controlled his glider by swinging his legs about: in other words it was an early *hang-glider*. Lilienthal even built an artificial hill, 15 metres high, near Berlin, and made about 2000 flights before he was killed in a gliding accident in 1896. His work was carried on by a British engineer called Percy Pilcher and an American, Octave Chanute, who also built hang-gliders.

Gliders have improved beyond recognition, but in still air they can only fly 'downhill' from their starting point so they often use a long tow-line to lift them high into the sky like a kite, or they make use of powered aircraft to tow them into the air. During the Second World War troop-carrying gliders were towed behind bombers and transport aircraft. In this way troops could be moved very quickly and even landed behind the enemy's line of defence.

Today, gliding is an international sport with clubs all over the world. A modern glider is one of the most graceful flying machines, with long slender wings and a smoothly curved body. Its surface is polished to a mirror-like finish in an effort to reduce air friction or drag. For many years gliders were made of wood and fabric but in recent years light aluminium alloys and plastics have taken over. The successful pilot stays in the air by seeking out up-currents of air from slopes or thermals. This requires considerable skill and the pilot must study cloud formations and meteorological conditions.

The aeroplane: early days

To convert a hang-glider, such as the one used by Otto Lilienthal, into an aeroplane needed two important innovations. A lightweight engine driving a propeller was needed, together with a method of controlling the aircraft in flight which was more reliable than the pilot swinging his legs about. Several pioneers achieved the first part but the second proved to be more difficult and it was the brothers Wilbur and Orville Wright who solved this problem using gliders and a wind tunnel.

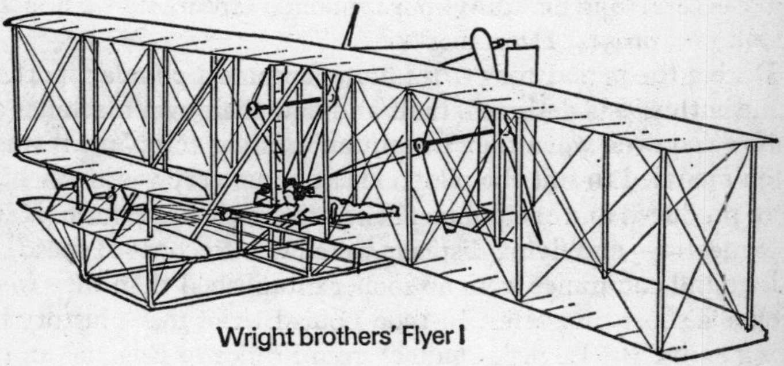

Wright brothers' Flyer I

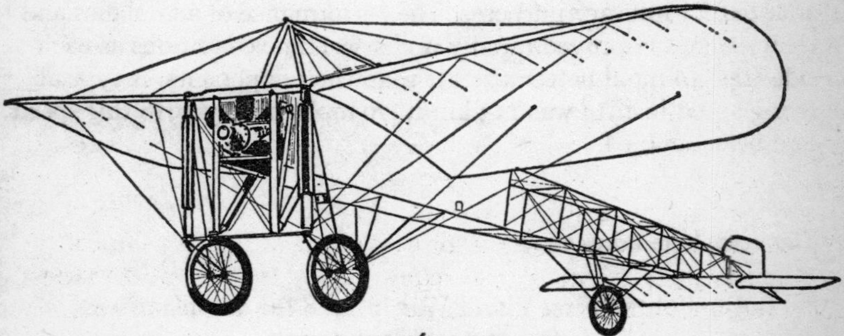

Louis Blériot's Type XI

Two remarkable aeroplanes

On 17th December 1903, Wilbur and Orville Wright made their first historic flights using a biplane powered by a petrol engine of their own design. The original 'Flyer' made four flights, the longest lasting just 59 seconds. A new 'Flyer' was built in 1904 and this made about eighty flights including simple manoeuvres and a complete circuit of the field. The longest flight achieved was 5 minutes 4 seconds. During the following year 'Flyer' No 3 made several longer flights – one lasting 38 minutes 3 seconds. It was not until April 1908 that their nearest rival exceeded 5 minutes for the first time, so when Wilbur demonstrated the latest 'Flyer' – or Model A – in France, observers were astonished by its performance. After several long flights Wilbur remained airborne for 2 hours 20 minutes on 31st December 1908.

During the period 1903–1914 flying became a popular sport. Some enthusiasts designed, built and flew their own machines as a hobby and even when they bought an existing aeroplane it was often modified to suit the pilot's ideas. Some very weird machines were produced and the public flocked to see them perform. Many race meetings and flying displays were held. Records of speed, height and endurance were no sooner established than they were broken a short time later. In 1909 Louis Blériot made history by flying across the English Channel from France to England and in 1911 the first officially sponsored airmail service was introduced between Hendon and Windsor.

Just when aeroplanes were emerging as a practical means of transport the First World War broke out and they were hastily adapted for military purposes. The performance of aeroplanes and their engines improved rapidly under wartime conditions as each side tried to build better aircraft than their opponents. A typical flying speed in 1914 was 113 km/h (70 mph) but by 1918 this speed had been doubled.

The aeroplane takes shape

By the end of the First World War in 1918 the aeroplane had emerged as a reliable flying machine and most designs used the same basic layout. This was called a *tractor biplane* because it had two wings and an engine in the nose of the aircraft which pulled it

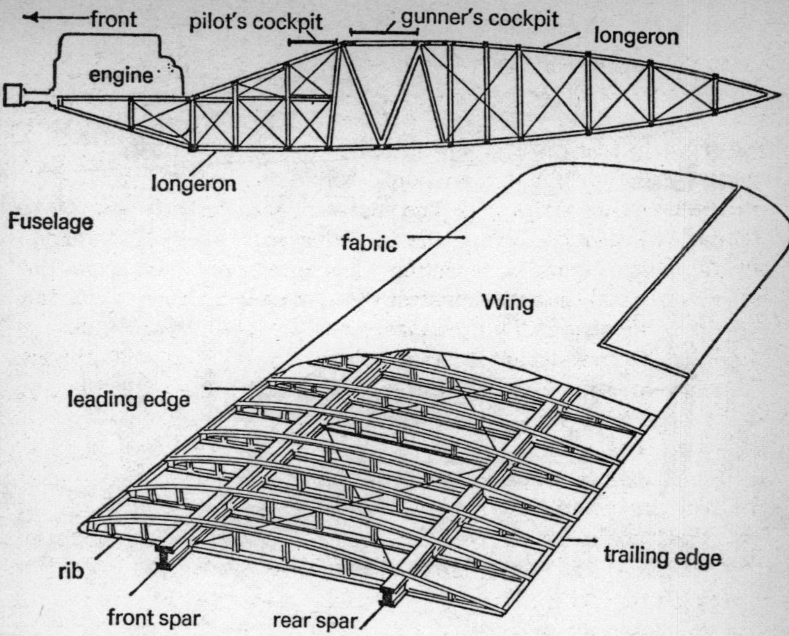

Beneath the skin of a First World War plane

through the air. Some earlier designs had been produced with an engine and propeller behind the pilot and this layout was called a *pusher*. Although the biplane was by far the most popular wing arrangement in 1918, it had been closely rivalled during the war by the monoplane and the triplane.

A typical aircraft of this period was the Bristol F.2B Fighter which arrived in France during 1917 and remained in service long after the war had finished. It had two wings, one above and one below the *fuselage*. The wings were separated by *struts* and braced by an array of wires. A Rolls-Royce Falcon engine was mounted in the nose and this drove a two-bladed wooden propeller. The F.2B carried a crew of two – both in open cockpits. The pilot sat in the forward cockpit while the observer/gunner sat behind him facing backwards and armed with one or two movable machine guns. The pilot also had a machine gun fixed to fire forwards through the propeller. At the rear of the fuselage was the tail unit consisting of the vertical *fin* and *rudder* and the horizontal *tailplane* and *elevator*. The *undercarriage* consisted of two wheels and a skid.

Aircraft of the First World War

Fokker E1 monoplane

Vickers FB5 Gun Bus, pusher biplane

Fokker Dr1 triplane

Bristol F2B biplane

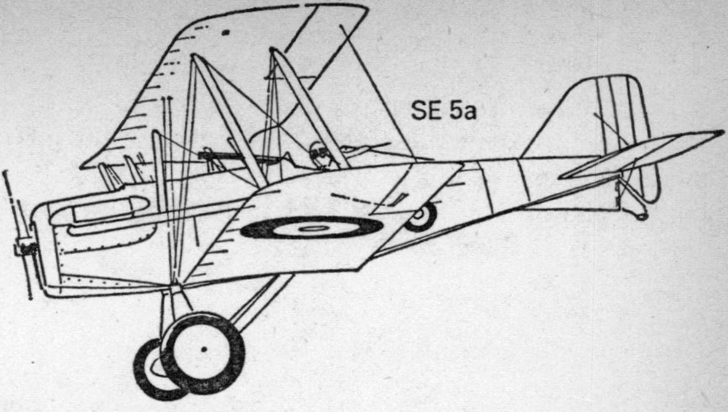

SE 5a

Spad S13

Sopwith Camel

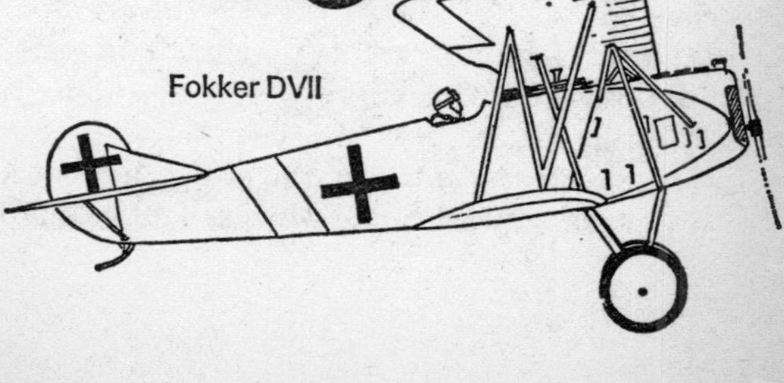

Fokker DVII

Between the wars from 1918 to 1939 the biplane remained the most common design, but by the 1930s its supremacy was being challenged by the monoplane. New methods of construction using metal structures enabled faster monoplanes to be built in ever increasing numbers and the biplane almost disappeared during the early years of the Second World War.

From sticks and string to stainless steel

When we look at a modern aircraft it is not easy to see how it is constructed – all we see is the external skin. By comparison early flying machines displayed parts of their skeletons for all to see. They were sometimes called 'stick and string' aeroplanes but 'wood and wire' would have been more accurate. The framework was manufactured from bamboo, spruce or ash and this was braced by both internal and external wires which could be tightened by *turnbuckles*. The need for wire bracing can be demonstrated by taking four equal lengths of wood and making them into a square using just one nail at each corner – the square has no rigidity. If two pieces of string are laid across the two diagonals and tied to the nails the square becomes rigid.

A tough fabric rather like canvas was used to cover the wings, tail unit and sometimes the fuselage. This fabric was painted with *dope* (a kind of varnish) to make it shrink and give a tight, smooth surface. The fuselage of a typical 1918 aeroplane such as the Bristol F.2B Fighter was a very simple structure. It resembled a long box with a spruce *longeron* running from nose to tail at each corner. Cross members and wire bracing completed the framework which was then covered with fabric. The main strength of the wings came from two spruce beams or *spars* which ran from tip to tip, while the shape of the wing section was produced by lightweight *ribs* running at right angles to the spars. Again the framework was fabric covered.

Over the years, improvements were made to increase the strength of aircraft structures. One improvement was to use thin plywood for the covering instead of fabric. The plywood was glued to the framework, so increasing the overall strength because plywood could carry some of the loading whereas fabric could not. This

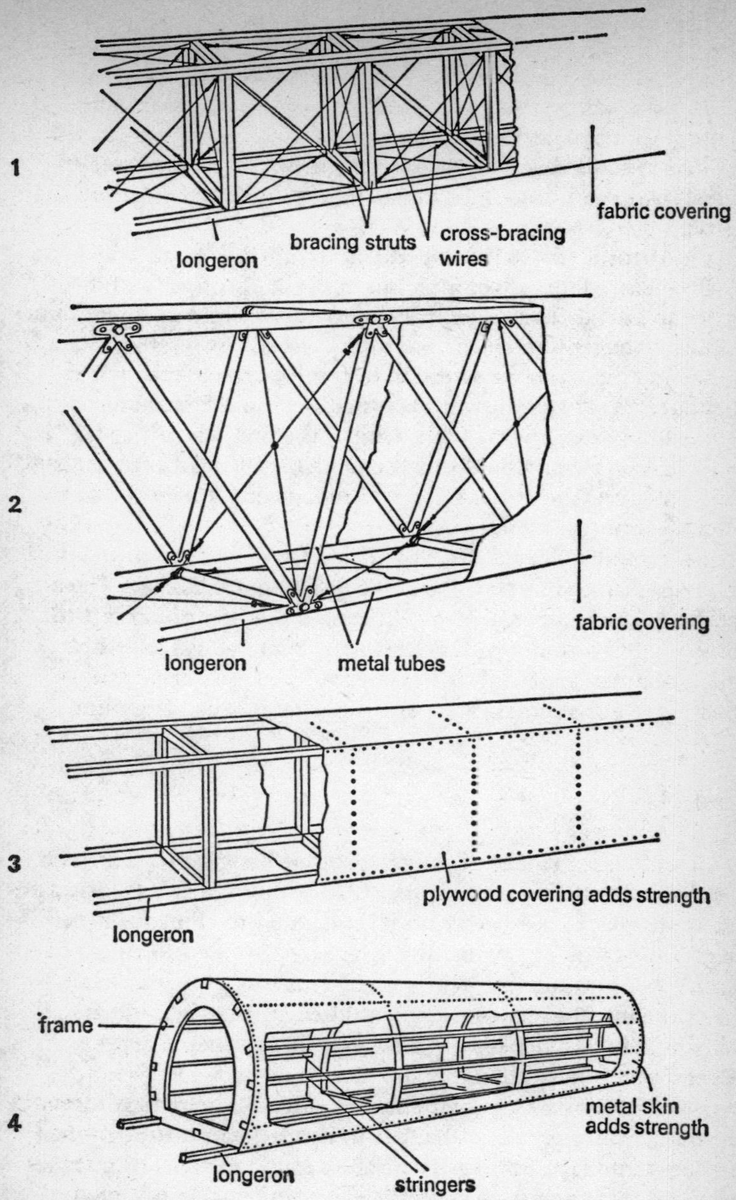

How aeroplanes are built
1 'Stick and string' – wood, wire and fabric. 2 Metal tubes and fabric. 3 Wood: stressed skin. 4 Metal: stressed skin

arrangement was called *stressed-skin* construction because the plywood skin was carrying some of the *stresses* and *strains*. Another improvement introduced metal fittings at highly-loaded joints and in some cases the wooden framework was completely replaced by one built up from metal tubes – but the fabric and wires remained.

By the 1930s a new metal called Duralumin was being widely used. It consisted mainly of aluminium but had copper and magnesium added. This *aluminium alloy* was as light as aluminium but much stronger – in fact it was almost as strong as steel. Some aircraft were built using a Duralumin framework covered with fabric, but a great step forward was made when a Duralumin stressed-skin structure was built. One of the first aircraft to be built using this new method was the Douglas DC-3 airliner of 1935. The robust structure of the DC-3 was renowned all over the world and several are still flying.

Aluminium alloy stressed-skin aircraft are still common today but very high speed aircraft have brought about a change. The air resistance at high supersonic speeds causes the skin of aircraft to become very hot, so hot in fact that aluminium alloys lose their strength and new materials are necessary. The answer to this problem is to use stainless steel or a new metal called titanium.

Controls

Otto Lilienthal's glider of 1891 was a simple hang-glider which he controlled by swinging his legs about. If he swung his legs forward it made the glider nose-heavy, so it dived, and to climb he swung his legs backwards. By swinging his legs to one side he could make the glider bank round in a gentle turn. This was a very simple method of control and, with some practice, it was very effective but it would not have been good enough for a powered aeroplane.

Several pioneers studied this problem of control and tried to improve on Lilienthal's weight-shifting. Movable control surfaces were the answer and one of the first to be used was a *rudder* – just like a ship's rudder it swung the aircraft round to the left or right (*yawing*). Another obvious control surface emerged called an *elevator* which was rather like a rudder turned on its side so that it

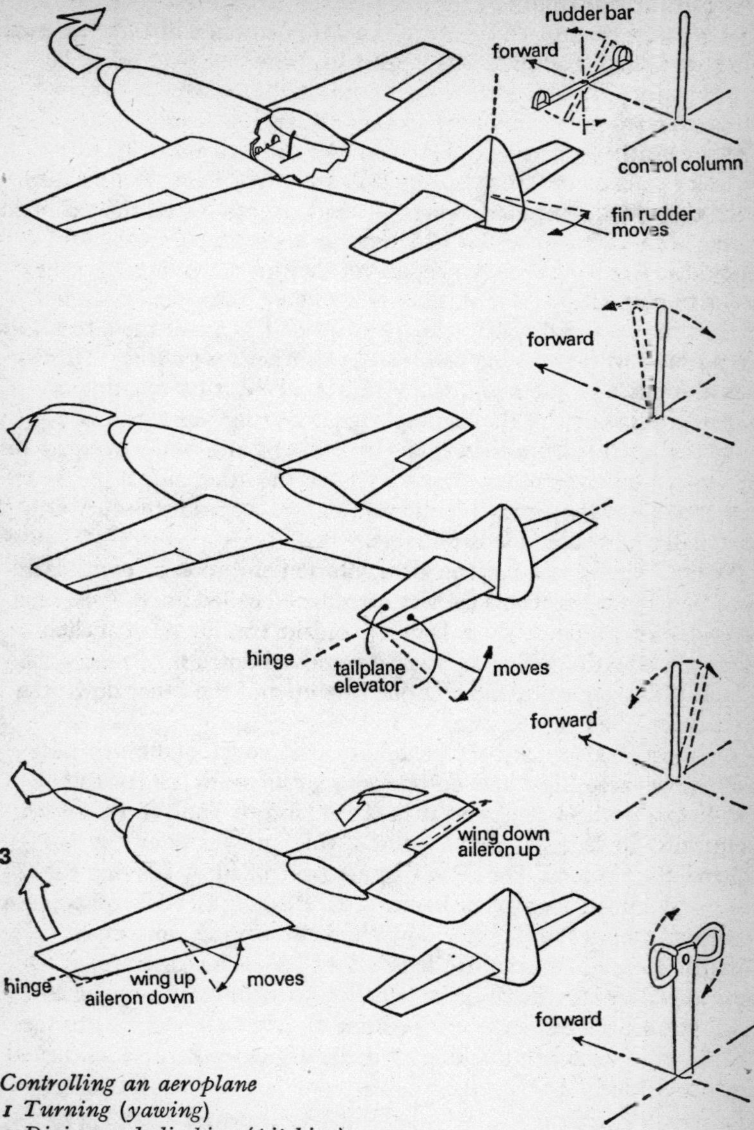

Controlling an aeroplane
1 Turning (yawing)
2 Diving and climbing (pitching)
3 Banking (rolling)

controlled the up and down movement of the aircraft (*pitching*). Today these control surfaces are usually positioned at the rear end of the fuselage. The rudder is hinged to a fixed vertical *fin* while the elevators are hinged to a horizontal *tailplane*. But the early pioneers tried many different arrangements. For instance, the Wright brothers' first aeroplane had two rudders at the rear and two elevators at the front but no fin and no tailplane. Before they built their first aeroplane, however, the Wrights tested their control surfaces on a biplane glider which they sometimes flew as a kite. They discovered that they needed yet another form of control in order to turn effectively. With only a rudder, the aircraft tended to slew round and fly crabwise. They needed to make the aircraft *bank* round with one wing down and the other up (*rolling*). This was a difficult problem and the Wrights solved it by twisting or *warping* the wings. If the leading edge of a wing was raised this increased the lift from that wing. By twisting the wings from tip to tip the lift on one side increased while on the other side it decreased – so the aircraft banked. This was a great step forward and made controlled flight possible.

Wing-warping was not the ideal solution and soon afterwards a simpler wing control surface was introduced called an *aileron*. This consisted of a hinged control surface on the trailing edge of each wing near the tip. When an aileron is moved down it increases the lift on that wing so by moving one side up and the other down the aircraft can be made to bank or roll.

On most modern aircraft the ailerons are controlled by turning a cut-down steering wheel on the *control column* in the cockpit. Turning the wheel clockwise makes the aircraft bank to the right. Some aircraft have a control column which moves sideways to control the ailerons. The elevators are controlled by moving the control column forwards or backwards. Pushing the control column forwards moves the elevator down and the aircraft nose dives. Finally, the rudder is controlled by foot pedals mounted on a hinged *rudder bar*. Moving the left foot forward and the right foot back swings the rudder to the left and the aircraft will yaw to the left, but for a smooth banking turn the wheel would also be turned anti-clockwise.

Petrol engines

The origins of the petrol engine can be traced back to the seventeenth century when Christiaan Huygens and Denis Papan experimented with an engine in which gunpowder was exploded inside a *cylinder* and the explosion moved a *piston*. Because the explosion takes place inside the cylinder this is called an *internal combustion engine*. Nearly two centuries passed before a working internal combustion engine emerged.

It was in 1860 that a French engineer, Etienne Lenoir, produced the first successful internal combustion engine in which a mixture of gas and air was ignited inside the cylinder by a spark. Lenoir's *gas engine* was an immediate successs for use in workshops and factories. Several improvements to increase the efficiency of gas engines followed but they were not very suitable for powering aircraft because they were slow running and they needed a supply of gas.

Eventually it became clear that petrol fumes or *vapour* could replace gas. In 1881 Gottlieb Daimler assisted by his friend Wilhelm Maybach tackled this problem and by 1885 they had a petrol engine working. Daimler offered the engine to his former employers but they turned it down. Undeterred, Daimler fitted his engine into a primitive motor cycle. In the same year another German engineer Karl Benz, working separately from Daimler, produced a three-wheeled car with a petrol engine. The following year Daimler produced a four-wheeled car with a high-speed petrol engine and this engine can be claimed to be the forerunner of modern motor car and aircraft engines.

The petrol engine was not the only source of power available for early airships and aeroplanes because steam engines and electric motors were also being used with some success. Then during the early years of the twentieth century the petrol engine improved and became widely used for cars and aeroplanes. Daimler's first engine had just one cylinder but most of the successful aero engines had two or more. Many cylinder arrangements were tried but the one chosen by the Wright brothers had four, one behind the other or *in-line*. The four pistons moved to and fro inside the cylinders and were connected to a *crankshaft* which rotated. The Wrights fitted two pusher propellers to drive their aeroplane

Petrol engines

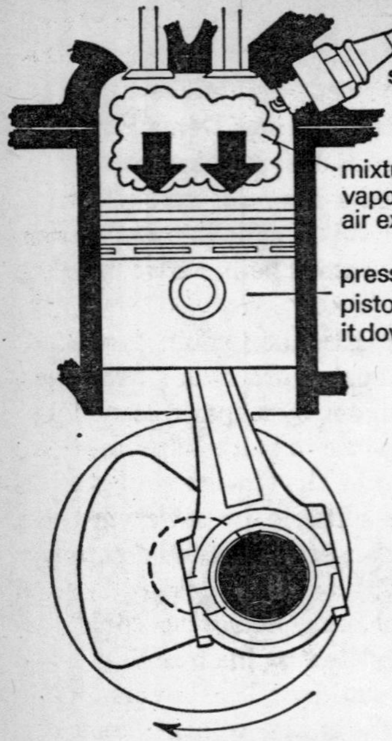

4-cylinder in-line engine used by the Wright brothers for their model A

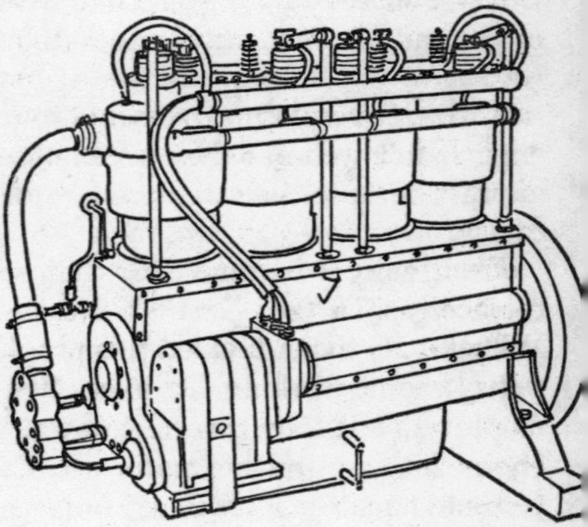

Engine cylinder layouts

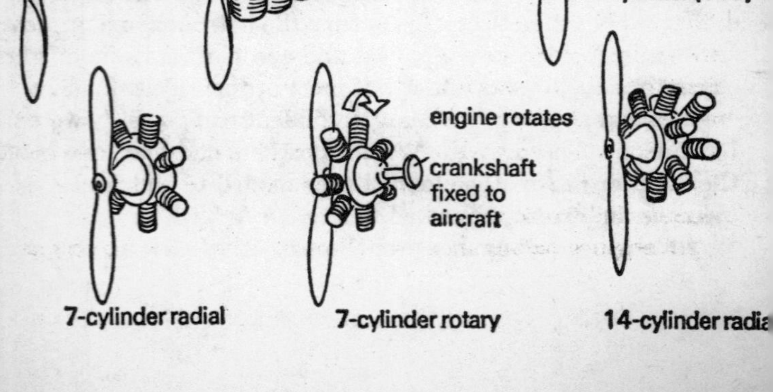

through the air and these were driven by bicycle chains from the crankshaft. Most designers fitted a propeller to an extension of the crankshaft and mounted the engine in the nose of the aeroplane. In-line engines sometimes had six or even eight cylinders but this arrangement resulted in a very long engine. A more compact engine could be built by arranging the cylinders around a short crankshaft. As the cylinders radiated from the crankshaft this was called a *radial* engine and once again the propeller rotated with the crankshaft. A very unusual engine was produced in France just before the First World War. It looked like a radial engine but the whole engine rotated around the crankshaft which was fixed to the aeroplane: the propeller was attached to the rotating engine. This arrangement created many problems but after these were overcome the *rotary* engine was a great success.

Petrol engines would become too hot if they were not cooled and, like most motor cars, the in-line aero engines were cooled by water flowing through a radiator. Radial and rotary engines were usually cooled by air flowing over their cylinders and these *air-cooled* engines can be recognised by the fins on their cylinders which increase the effectiveness of the cooling air. Between the two World Wars there was great rivalry between Britain's two leading aero engine companies. Rolls-Royce preferred in-line, liquid-cooled engines while Bristol favoured air-cooled, radial engines. Both companies made some very successful engines, for example the Rolls-Royce Merlin in the Spitfire and the Bristol Hercules which powered the later Wellington bombers.

Jet engines

The first aeroplane to fly using a jet engine was the German Heinkel He 178 in August 1939, some two years before the first British jet engine was ready for flight testing. However, the Heinkel's engine was not developed for production aircraft, whereas many of the early British and American jet aircraft were powered by engines based on the British design developed by a Flying Instructor in the RAF called Frank Whittle (later to become Sir Frank Whittle).

Jet engines belong to a whole family of engines called *gas*

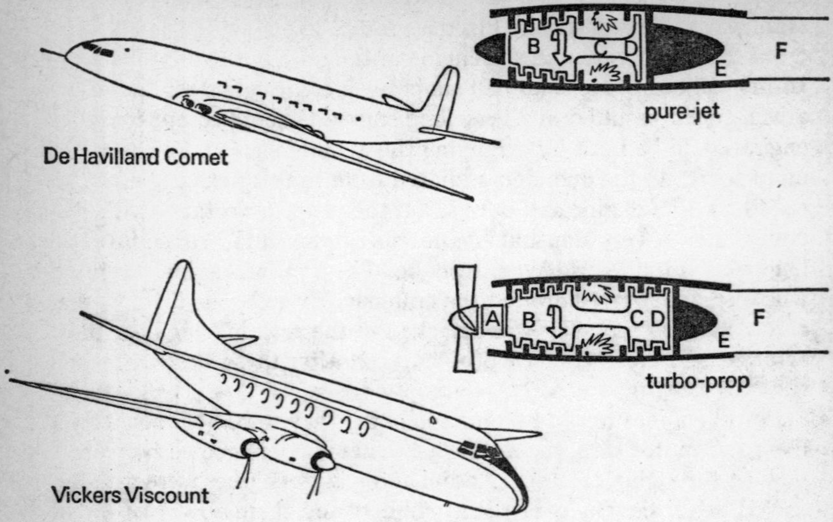

Jet engines: (A) gearbox; (B) compressor; (C) combustion chamber; (D) turbine; (E) jet-pipe; (F) jet.

turbines. In a gas turbine, air is drawn into the engine and compressed by an air compressor, then it passes to a combustion section into which fuel is sprayed and ignited. The fuel burns fiercely and produces hot gases at a high temperature and pressure. These gases emerge from the rear of the engine as a jet. However, before emerging they pass through a *turbine* (a high-speed windmill), and this turbine drives the compressor. If a larger turbine is fitted it can be used to drive a propeller in addition to the compressor, and this is called a *turbo-prop* or *prop-jet* engine.

In the years just after the Second World War Britain decided to design airliners powered by the relatively new jet or turbo-prop engines. The de Havilland Comet and Vickers Viscount were built and eventually made their mark, cutting flight times and providing a very comfortable flight. The popularity of the turbo-prop engine was short-lived but jet-engined airliners are still being produced in large numbers.

Wheels, floats and skis

Once an aeroplane is in the air its wheels or other type of *undercarriage* are just so much dead weight, but during take-off or landing they are, of course, vital. The first glider to fly successfully had a very unusual undercarriage – it had legs! Otto Lilienthal carried his glider and ran downhill to become airborne. Then at the end of his flight he landed on his legs. Percy Pilcher followed Lilienthal's lead for take-off but he went one better when it came to landing. His glider was fitted with wheels and these were supported on springs so the impact of landing was taken by the springs. This was the first sprung undercarriage in the world and the idea has since been incorporated in most aeroplanes. The Wright brothers devised an unusual undercarriage arrangement for their aeroplanes or 'Flyers' as they called them. The Flyers did not have wheels, they had two skids. For take-off the skids were placed on little trolleys which ran on wooden rails. Once the Flyer became airborne it lifted off the trolleys and they stayed on the ground. The Flyer then landed on its skids, which was rather bumpy! Later Flyers were helped into the air by a catapult device.

European aviators preferred wheels, for example the monoplane designed and flown by Louis Blériot on the first cross-Channel flight in 1909 had two wheels at the front and one at the rear. Blériot's undercarriage was sprung with coiled steel springs but many other designers lashed their wheels to the undercarriage structure with very strong rubber bands or *bungees*. These absorbed the shock but the aircraft did tend to bounce. Many of the early aircraft used a *skid* at the rear rather than a wheel and this acted as a brake after the aircraft had landed – there were no other brakes! On take-off the tail soon lifted off the ground so the skid did not slow the aircraft down.

In the 1930s undercarriages were greatly improved by two new types of springing. One used a wheel which had springs inside it and the other used a sprung leg called an *oleo*. To demonstrate an oleo, take a bicycle pump and place a finger over the hole where the air emerges. Now if the handle is pushed in, it is resisted by the springiness of the trapped air. An oleo works in a similar fashion. These improvements made landing much more comfortable but undercarriages were still a double problem: they were heavy

Wheels

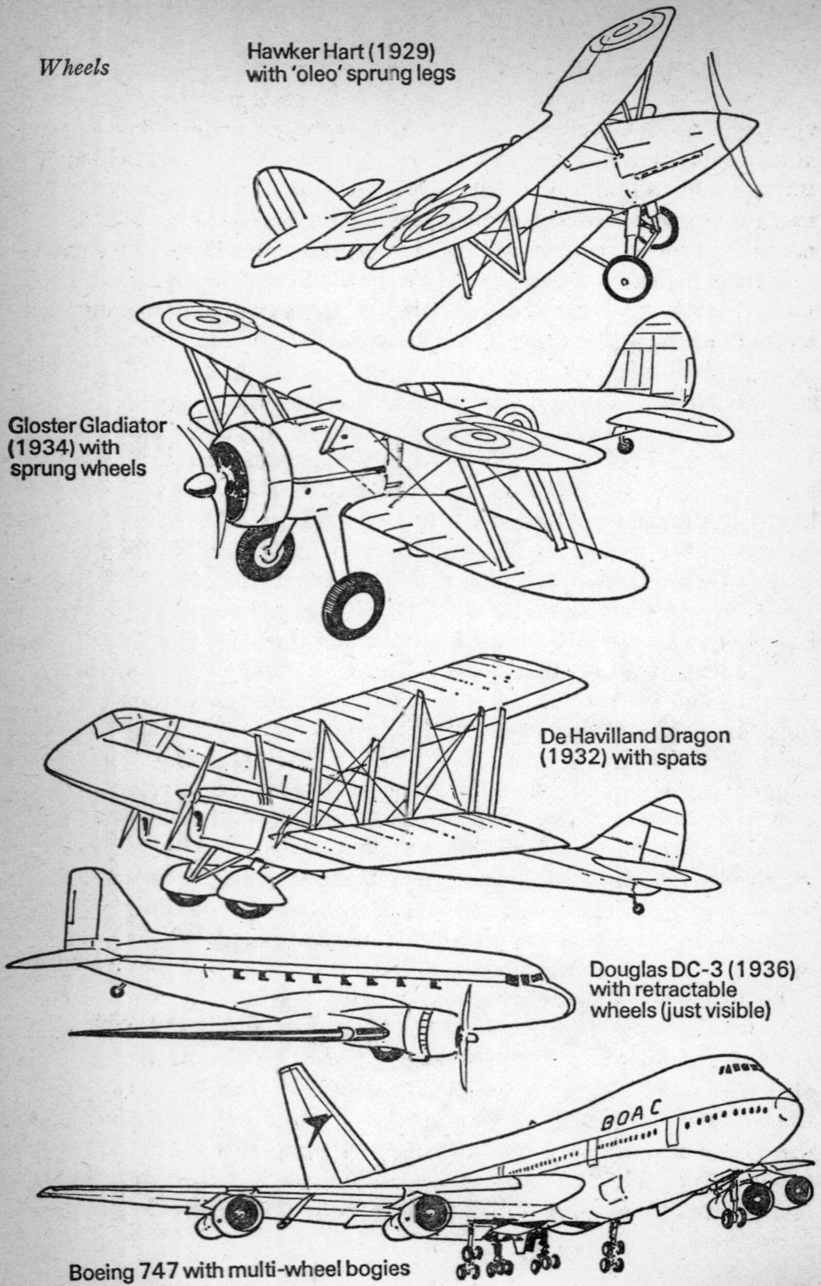
Hawker Hart (1929)
with 'oleo' sprung legs
Gloster Gladiator
(1934) with
sprung wheels
De Havilland Dragon
(1932) with spats
Douglas DC-3 (1936)
with retractable
wheels (just visible)
BOAC
Boeing 747 with multi-wheel bogies

and they caused a considerable amount of air resistance or drag. The drag was reduced by designing streamlined legs and fitting sleek *spats* over the wheels. Then in the late 1930s undercarriages which *retracted* inside the wing or fuselage were introduced and this improvement eliminated the drag problem but added weight. A major change in recent years has been to use multi-wheel *bogies* to carry the ever increasing weights of aircraft using existing runways.

In 1910 a French aeroplane with a very different kind of undercarriage made its first flight. Henri Fabre's peculiar looking flying machine was fitted with floats and it took off from water.

Seaplanes

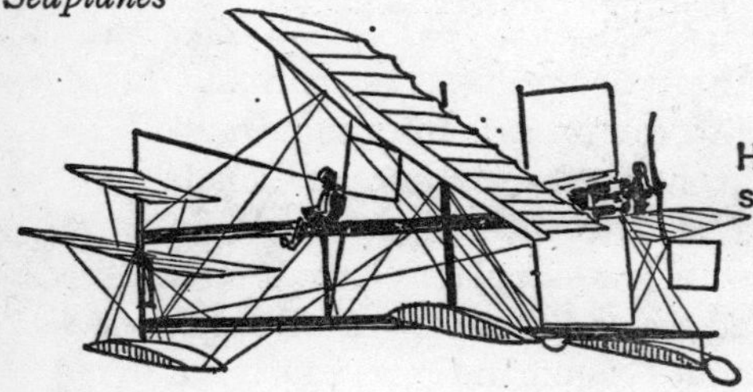

Henri Fabre's seaplane (1910)

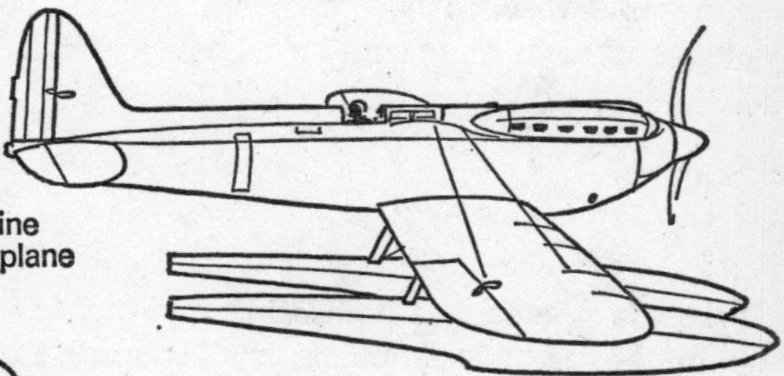

Supermarine S.6B floatplane (1931)

Short Empire flying boat (1936)

Grumman Goose amphibian (1937)

Many *seaplanes* followed and perhaps the most spectacular were the racing *floatplanes* flown in the famous Schneider Trophy races in the late 1920s. In 1931 Britain won the Trophy outright and the Supermarine S.6B went on to break the world air-speed record at 655 km/h (406.99 mph). Larger seaplanes were often designed as *flying boats* in which the fuselage or *hull* floated on the water and small steadying floats were fitted at the wing tips. In the early days of long-distance flying, seaplanes were very convenient because a suitable stretch of water could usually be found whereas *aerodromes* were few and far between. In the 1930s Britain's Imperial Airways flew both landplanes and flying boats and their Short Empire flying boats of 1937 were very popular with passengers and crew.

For flights in Arctic and Antarctic areas skis are normally fitted instead of wheels so the aircraft can operate from snow or ice. Canadian *bush* pilots flying in the northern wastes of Canada fly rugged aeroplanes which can be fitted with either wheels, floats or skis, depending on conditions. A few aeroplanes have been designed to operate from both land and sea and these are called *amphibians*. One of the most successful is the Grumman Goose which is a flying boat with retractable wheels. Helicopters with floats can easily be made amphibious whereas some land-based helicopters have just skids – like the Wright Flyer!

Instruments

When the Wright brothers made the world's first flight their aeroplane did not have any instruments at all whereas a modern airliner or jet fighter has a pilot's seat absolutely surrounded by instruments. Over the years the need for instruments to help a pilot has grown as aircraft have become larger, faster and generally more complicated. In the early days of flying pilots were said to 'fly by the seat of their pants' because they relied on their own judgment to decide whether they were climbing or diving, for example. In cloudy conditions this could be very difficult and even dangerous so instruments were invented to help out.

Some of the first instruments gave the pilot information about his engine such as the engine speed, for it was important not to run the engine too fast or it would seize up. Then he needed a fuel

A pitot head. By comparing the pressure at A with the static pressure at B, the airspeed can be measured.

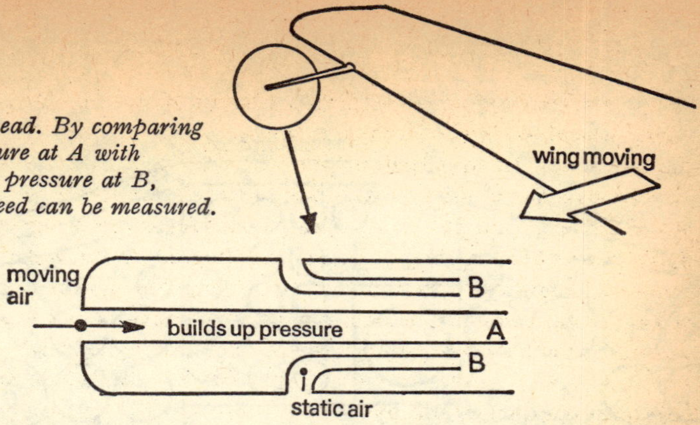

gauge to tell him how much petrol was in his tank. Now these instruments were also used by sports cars but when it came to measuring speed the automobile speedometer was no help because it was driven by the wheels. When an aeroplane is flying, its speed is measured by comparing the air pressure entering a forward-facing tube with the pressure of a sideways-facing tube. This *pitot head* is connected to an *air speed indicator* in the cockpit which gives the pilot his speed through the air. Now there is a problem because the air might also be moving; for example, the aircraft could be flying into a headwind of 30 km/h (19 mph). If the airspeed indicator showed a speed of 100 km/h (62 mph) then the aircraft's speed over the ground would be only 70 km/h (43 mph). To cope with speeds greater than the speed of sound (*Mach* 1) modern aircraft also carry a machmeter which indicates the mach number (Mach 2 would be twice the speed of sound).

A pilot needs to know the height at which his aircraft is flying and this is measured by an *altimeter* which operates by measuring the air pressure, which decreases as height is increased. But this method only measures height above the point of departure and if a high mountain range has to be crossed this might not be accurate enough. A radio altimeter overcame this problem by sending a signal to the ground and back: the timing of this signal gives the aircraft's height above the ground. A third height instrument is also carried and this is called a *rate of climb indicator* or vertical speed indicator. This tells the pilot his speed of ascent or descent which is not always obvious. A pilot might think he is flying along straight and level but a thermal could be carrying his aircraft upwards.

An aircraft's instrument panel

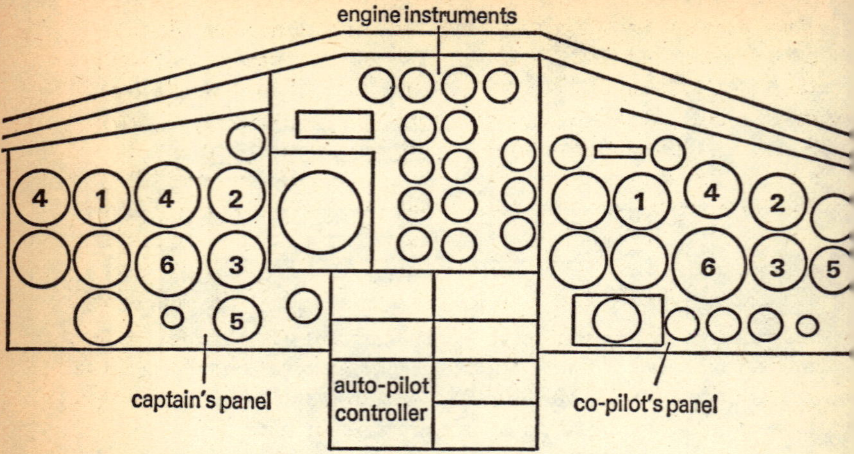

1 airspeed/mach indicator
2 altimeter
3 vertical speed indicator
4 artificial horizon/attitude director
5 turn and slip indicator
6 gyro compass indicator

Flying in thick cloud presents problems and it has been known for a pilot to emerge from a cloud upside down thinking he was still the right way up. Our senses are unreliable, but a *gyroscope* does not lose its sense of direction and so pilots rely upon this fact to guide them. If a pilot cannot see the horizon his gyro-controlled *artificial horizon* shows him whether he is climbing or diving and whether he is banking. He also has a *turn and slip* or *turn and bank* indicator which measures the tightness of a turn.

Most aircraft carry a *magnetic compass* to help the pilot fly on his correct course but a magnetic compass can be unreliable (especially near the poles). To back up the magnetic compass a *gyro compass* or directional gyro is carried. A further series of gyros were eventually linked together to control an aircraft and keep it flying on a straight and level course. This *autopilot* was well established by the outbreak of war in 1939 and to the RAF crews on long missions 'George' the automatic pilot was a godsend. Today's aircraft carry very advanced instruments and computers but most of them are just improved versions of the simple instruments of the early days.

Flaps and slats: STOL

Some aircraft are designed to fly slowly at all times but all aeroplanes have to fly slowly some of the time, namely during take-off and landing. This creates a problem because one of the most important factors which produces lift from a wing is speed. So reducing the speed reduces the lift, yet the wing still has to support the weight of the aeroplane. To compensate extra lift is therefore needed, so the designers have to study the other factors affecting lift. These are air density, wing area, angle of incidence and the wing shape. The density of air cannot be changed but increasing the size of the wing might be considered. The angle of incidence can be increased by flying the aeroplane in a nose-up attitude, but if this angle is increased too much then the flow of air becomes turbulent and the aeroplane drops out of the sky in a *stall*. So the final item to be considered is the wing shape or *aerofoil section*. A flat wing section gives only a little lift but a curved or *cambered* section increases the lift considerably. So the *flap* was devised to increase the camber of the lower surface of the wing.

Wing shapes: aerofoil sections

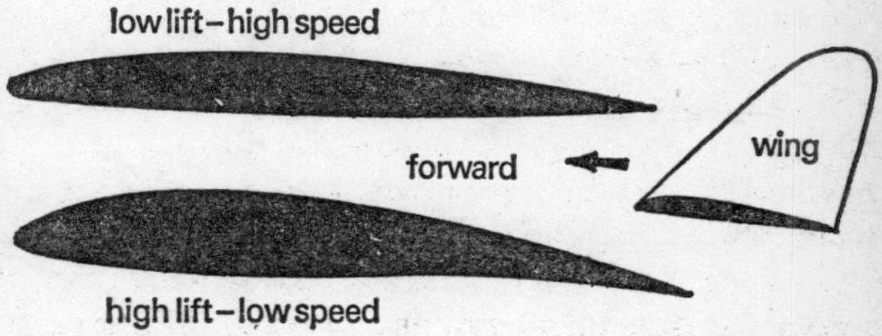

A number of flap designs have been tried out over the years ranging from a simple hinged flap or the split flap to the more complicated versions such as the slotted flap or the Fowler flap. The Fowler flap had a double advantage – it increased the camber and it moved out to increase the wing area. Lowering the flaps increases not only the lift but also the drag. Now this is a good

Wing flaps

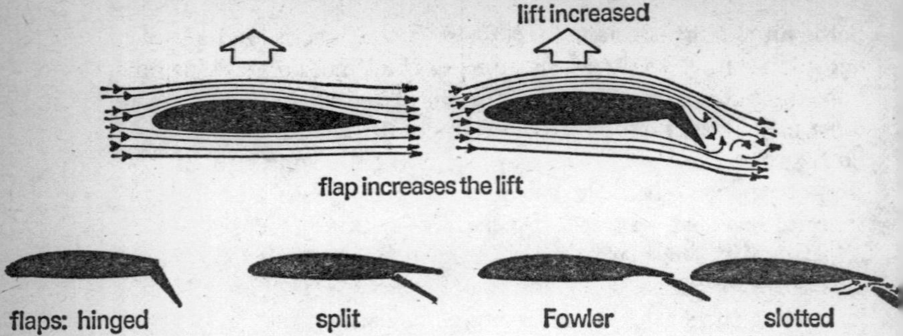

Slats, slots and drooping wings

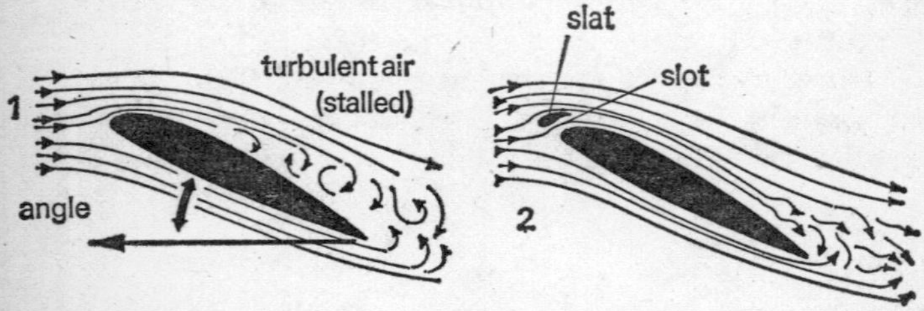

1 Wing stalls at large angle of incidence.
2 Slat and slot smooth out air and delay stall.

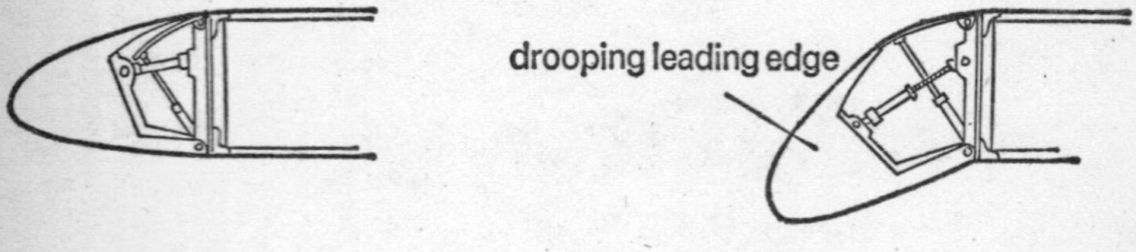

thing during a landing when the aeroplane is slowing down but not so good for take-off when the aeroplane is accelerating. Consequently a pilot lowers the flaps only part of the way for take-off.

In the 1920s a British aviation pioneer, Frederick Handley Page, developed another device to produce more lift from a wing at low speeds. It was called a *slat* and consisted of a mini-wing mounted along the leading edge leaving a *slot* between the slat and the wing. The Handley Page slat enabled a wing to fly with a much greater angle of incidence without stalling. The wings of modern jet airliners usually have flaps along part of the trailing edge plus a leading edge slat or drooping leading edge which increases the camber.

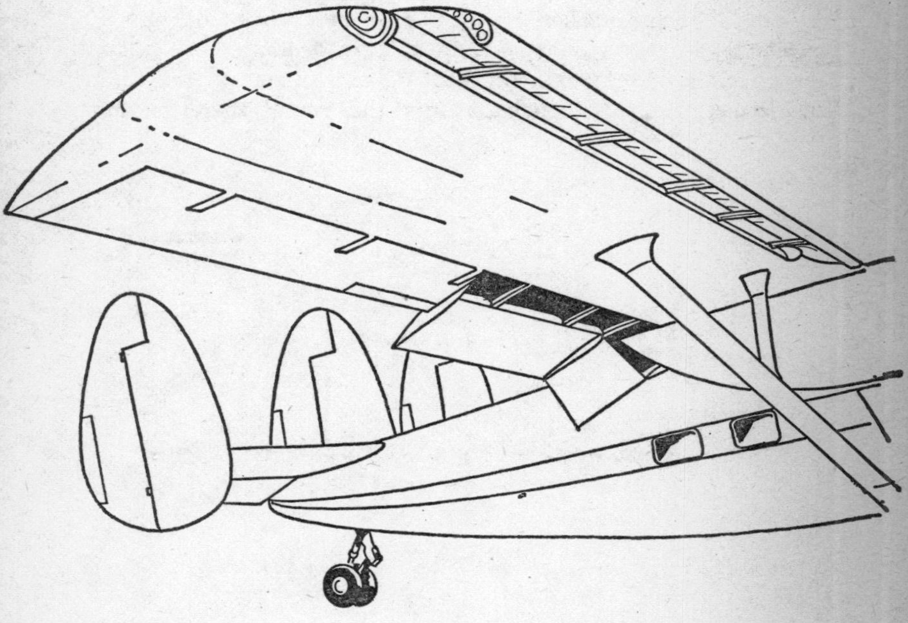

An early STOL aircraft, the Scottish Aviation Twin-Pioneer, showing the movable slats on the leading edge of the wing and the trailing edge flaps which increase the lift at slow speeds.

Special aircraft have been designed to operate from short landing strips in jungles or remote regions and these are now referred to as *STOL* aircraft (Short Take-Off and Landing). Naturally they include several high-lift devices and examples include the Westland Lysander of World War Two and the recent design from de Havilland Canada, the Dash 7.

VTOL aircraft

It took many years for aircraft designers to produce a really effective Vertical Take-Off and Landing, or *VTOL*, aircraft in order to dispense with large and costly aerodromes. The helicopter fulfils some of the requirements: it can certainly take-off vertically but the large rotor makes it difficult to produce a helicopter capable of high speeds. One solution involved using several small rotors (or large propellers) and a number of strange-looking machines appeared. Some of these had two or four engines mounted on a tilting wing: for take-off the wing and engines pointed upwards so the propellers lifted the aircraft off the ground, then the wing

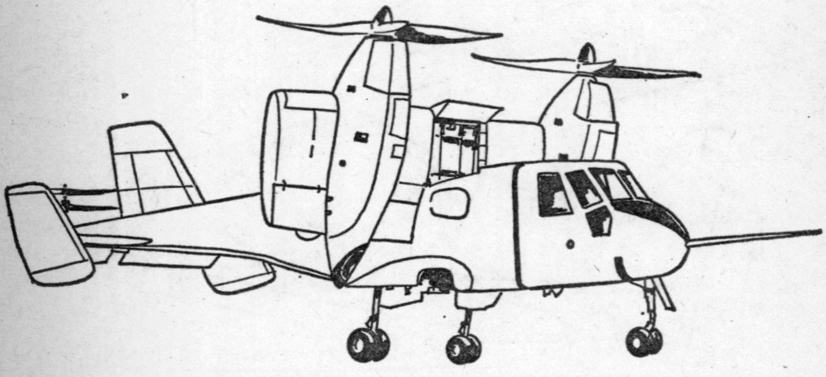

A convertiplane – the Canadair CL-84. The wing is tilted as shown for take-off and then rotated to the normal position in flight.

was tilted into the normal position with the engines pointing forwards and the *convertiplane* flew as a conventional aeroplane. Few progressed beyond the experimental stage.

The invention of the jet engine with its powerful thrust made VTOL aircraft a distinct possibility. In 1953 the Rolls-Royce 'Flying Bedstead' lifted into the air, powered by two Nene engines with their jets directed downwards. The Short SC-1 followed with four *lifting* engines and one other engine for forward propulsion, but this aircraft was only experimental – although its layout is favoured by some people for the airliner of the future. Another

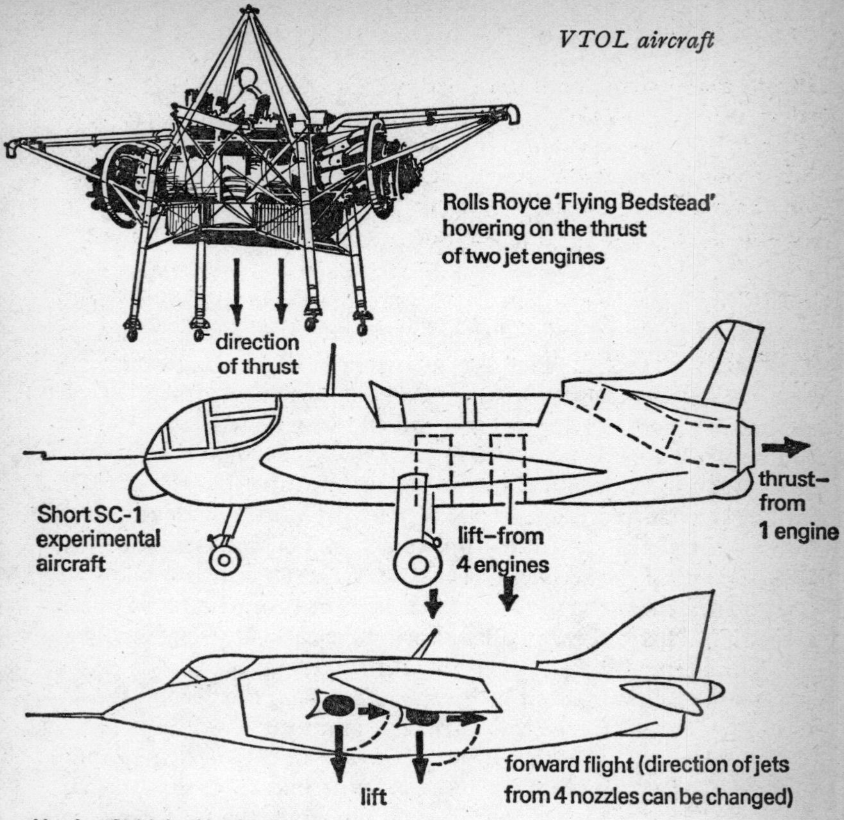

Hawker Siddeley Harrier fighter

variation is to change the direction of a jet between take-off and flight – either by tilting the engine or by deflecting the jet as it emerges from the engine. The most successful aircraft of this type is the British Hawker-Siddeley Harrier fighter flown by the RAF and other airforces. This has a single engine but its jet emerges from four movable nozzles, which point downwards for take-off or to the rear in flight.

There have been some weird and wonderful designs for VTOL aircraft produced in recent years but most of them are experimental and it will be many years before they carry passengers and freight.

Autogiros and helicopters

The idea of a helicopter is not new – Leonardo da Vinci sketched one in the fifteenth century. The problem was to produce a practical, reliable and efficient machine. As early as 1907 a crude form of helicopter lifted itself and a pilot vertically into the air, but it was only a short flight. A number of attempts were made during the following years but these flights were mere 'hops'.

In the 1920s, however, a great step forward was made when the Spanish engineer, Juan de la Cierva, invented the *autogiro*. Both the autogiro and the helicopter obtain their lifting power from a large horizontal rotor which acts as two or more rotating wings. The basic difference between the two flying machines lies in the method of driving this rotor. It is driven by an engine in a helicopter, but is free to rotate in an autogiro. In flight the rotor of an autogiro is blown round due to the forward speed of the aircraft. A petrol engine and propeller are usually fitted to provide this forward speed although autogiros were towed behind German U-boats during the Second World War. When an autogiro takes off it requires a short run to start the large rotor turning and of course a head wind helps. It can climb almost vertically, fly very slowly and land vertically. In 1935 the RAF received Cierva C.30 autogiros which were built in Britain and during the Second World War autogiros were used to test radar equipment.

The success of the autogiro encouraged helicopter designers and by 1937 the Germans had produced an experimental helicopter. It could not lift a great load, but it could remain in the air for over an hour and it was reasonably controllable. Controlling a helicopter in flight was a major problem for the early designers. A few years later in America, the first really practical helicopter was designed and flown by the Russian-born Igor Sikorsky. His VS.300 set the pattern for the majority of helicopters built since that date.

Sikorsky's helicopter had a large lifting rotor and a propeller at the tail facing sideways: both were driven by the same petrol engine. Without the propeller or small rotor the fuselage would have rotated in the opposite direction to the main rotor. Several Sikorsky designs were hurried into production and over 400 had been built by the end of the war. The Sikorsky layout of rotors has remained popular since these early days but several other layouts

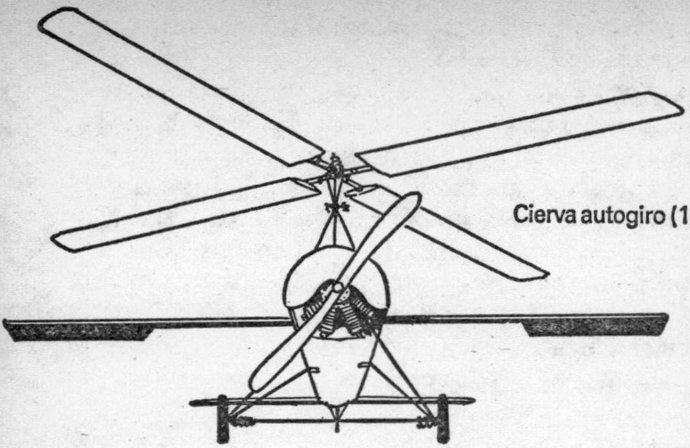

Cierva autogiro (1923)

Sikorsky's first successful helicopter (1942)

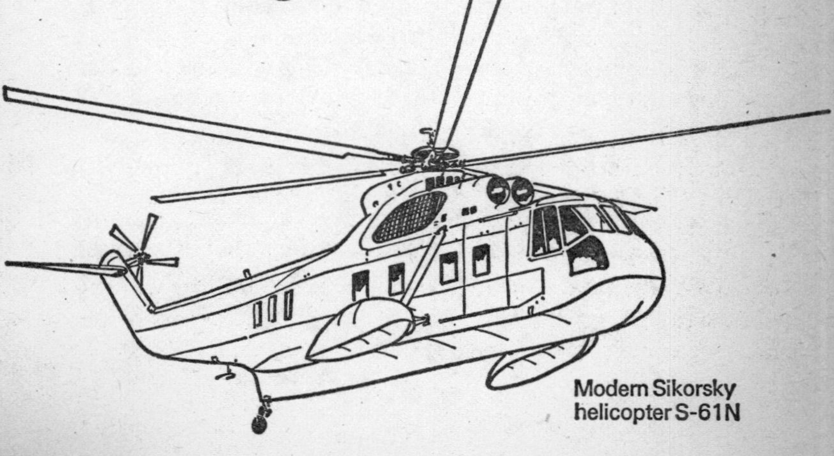

Modern Sikorsky helicopter S-61N

have emerged. For instance, two main rotors rotating in opposite directions eliminate the need for a tail rotor.

Almost every day helicopters are in the news, usually because they have rescued someone in distress. But in addition to their rescue missions helicopters are used as a means of transport, a lifeboat, a crane, an observation post, an ambulance, a lorry, an agricultural implement and a weapon of war. The secret of the helicopter's success lies in its ability to hover and operate from any small open space. But helicopters do have some disadvantages; for instance they are noisy. They are also expensive, both to buy and to operate, a fact which is largely due to their rotors and the complicated mechanism used to control them.

Hovercraft

The *hovercraft* was invented in the 1950s by a British electronics engineer, Christopher Cockerell, who was interested in boats as a hobby. He studied high-speed boats and the problem of water-resistance. To overcome this resistance he decided to separate the boat from the water by a cushion of air. It took him several years to invent a method of keeping a cushion of air under his experimental craft. Cockerell fitted a large fan, which would blow air into the space beneath the craft. To prevent this air from escaping he considered using rigid walls or curtains extending down to the surface of the water. But rigid walls would not be very effective over waves, as the air might escape, so Cockerell tried a flexible curtain of water but this proved to be heavy and not very practical. He eventually decided to use a curtain of high-pressure air ejected all round the edge of the craft. This curtain of air was angled downward and inward so that it provided, not only a wall, but also a supply of air for the cushion.

A full-size version of Cockerell's hovercraft was ordered from Saunders-Roe and in 1959 the SR-N1 appeared. It could fly at a height of 23 centimetres (9 inches) and travel at almost 50 km/h (31 mph). The success of the hovercraft was remarkable because, in just a few years, it changed from a scientific experiment to a practical vehicle. Even the aeroplane took almost twenty years to make this change.

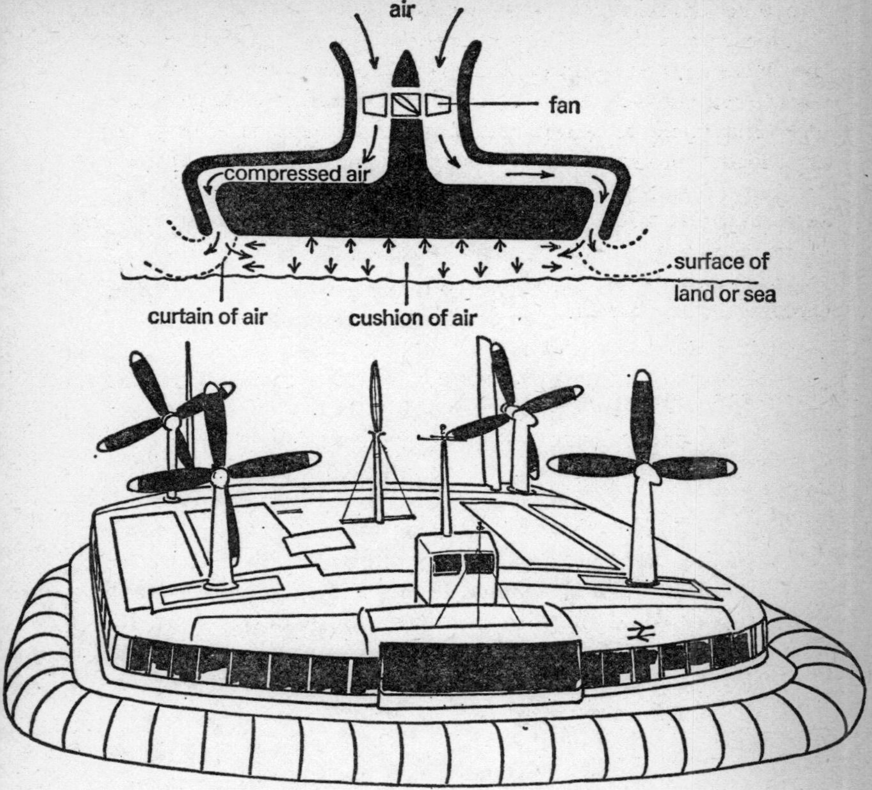

A hovercraft and how it works

Travelling on a cushion of air has many advantages and the hovercraft can travel faster than a conventional ship, which has to plough its way through the water. It can travel across ice, sand banks, shallows and rapids, marshland and weed-infested water. Many different variations of the hovercraft have been produced and most of them have some kind of inflatable rubber curtain instead of just air but they all float on a cushion of air. In fact they are sometimes called *cushion-craft* or even *ground-effect machines*.

3 Airlines

Passengers: the pioneering days

The first passengers to fly on an airline service were carried, not in aeroplanes, but in Zeppelins. These huge rigid airships were designed by the German Count Ferdinand von Zeppelin and could carry some twenty passengers in considerable comfort. Indeed on most flights a meal was served to the passengers. Between 1910 and 1914 almost 1600 flights were made between German cities covering a total of over 160,000 km (100,000 miles). Several Zeppelins were damaged in accidents but these were mainly on the ground and not a single passenger was injured. The outbreak of the First World War ended all hopes of further passenger services.

Soon after the war, in 1919, daily passenger flights between London and Paris were started. In contrast to the luxury of the Zeppelins, the passengers were carried in the tiny cabins of converted bombers. It was a cold and uncomfortable journey but it took a mere two and a half hours compared with the seven or eight hours by rail and steamer. Flying was very expensive and only the rich could afford to use this new form of transport. In a few years larger aircraft carrying more passengers were designed and these early airliners cut the cost of journeys. Year by year the airlines extended their services and by 1925 most of the European capitals were linked by air.

The next stage was to extend the air routes further afield, but to do this larger multi-engined airliners were needed and aerodromes had to be constructed along the routes. These routes were carefully planned to avoid regions where forced landings would be dangerous, such as mountain ranges or deserts. Some countries refused to let aircraft of other nations fly over their territory and they too had to be avoided. In 1929 Europe was linked with India and three years later a service to South Africa was started. By 1935 Australia could be reached by air in twelve days but many stops were made to refuel. The early airliners, such as the famous Handley Page HP.42, had a limited range and did not fly during the night. Year by year the performance of airliners improved and the journey times were reduced.

In the early days of air travel passengers were provided with thick coats, helmets and gloves. Inset: passenger cabin of a Zeppelin in 1910

Air travel today

Millions of people travel by air today, in fact on some routes more people fly than travel by surface transport. Flying has become a very easy way to travel. The first step is to buy a ticket and reserve a seat at the airline office or travel agents. This is a very simple operation which on the face of it requires only a few people behind the counter but behind the scenes there is a large staff checking reservations to ensure that the aircraft is not over-filled. People from many parts of the world may be wishing to reserve seats on the same aircraft, so a large computer system is used to keep a check on the empty seats.

When the day of the flight arrives, passengers travel to the airport where they *check-in*. Again this is a simple operation for passengers consisting of a few formalities such as having their baggage weighed. The airline staff then have to ensure that the luggage is loaded and that the aircraft is not overloaded. The flight number is called over the loudspeaker and after a short wait passengers are shepherded through the security search and, on international flights, their passports are checked. Passengers then board the waiting aircraft where the stewardess welcomes them aboard and inspects tickets. The captain will be making last minute checks having already studied the aircraft loading and the weather reports. When all the passengers are aboard and the doors closed the engines are started under the supervision of the ground crew and firemen. The captain then contacts the control tower by radio to ensure that it is safe for him to taxi the airliner out to the runway ready for take-off. Once in the air the captain is not free to fly where he pleases for there are special routes laid down by international agreement. By sticking to a known route the risk of collision is reduced for the sky is a busy place today. Radio and radar stations along the route enable the aircraft's position to be checked regularly. Eventually the airliner reaches its destination where once again a host of people are on hand to look after the passengers and the plane.

Airlines are always seeking to reduce journey times so the aircraft designers continue to design faster and faster machines. In recent years a great step forward has been made with supersonic airliners such as the Concorde which can fly at over 2000 km/h

(1300 mph). At this speed a passenger flying to the United States can reach his destination in only four hours – compared with the old flight time of eight to nine hours. This can be confusing because of the time difference between the two countries. For example, New York time is five hours behind London time, so if a supersonic airliner leaves London at 8 a.m. and takes four hours for its journey, it arrives in New York at 12 noon (London time), which is 7 a.m. in New York. The passenger has 'arrived' one hour before he left so he can have a second breakfast!

Airliners

Standing in the spectators' area at any large airport and looking out over the parked airliners reveals that they are almost all jets. The jet-age started in the 1950s and made a fairly slow start. Jet aircraft had been used during the Second World War but in its early days the jet engine was not very suitable for airliners because its fuel consumption was too high. Most of the airliner's load-carrying ability would have been taken up with fuel instead of fare-paying passengers. Gradually jet engines were improved and in 1952 Britain led the world with the de Havilland Comet airliner fitted with four de Havilland jet engines. Unfortunately on two occasions Comets crashed due to a structural weakness and the airliner had to be re-designed. In 1958 the new Comet 4 began services across the Atlantic and it was joined a few weeks later by a new American jet airliner, the Boeing 707. The days of the propeller-driven airliner were numbered.

For a short time European aircraft manufacturers led the way pioneering new layouts. For example, the Boeing 707 followed the layout of the old piston-engined airliners with four engines mounted on the wings but the Comet had its four engines buried inside the wing to reduce the drag. Another layout designed to produce a *cleaner* wing was introduced on the French Sud-Aviation Caravelle which had two engines attached to the sides of the fuselage near the tail. This arrangement was also used very successfully by the BAC One-Eleven. De Havilland followed the Comet with the Trident, a three-engined airliner which had one engine on each side of the rear fuselage and one on the top.

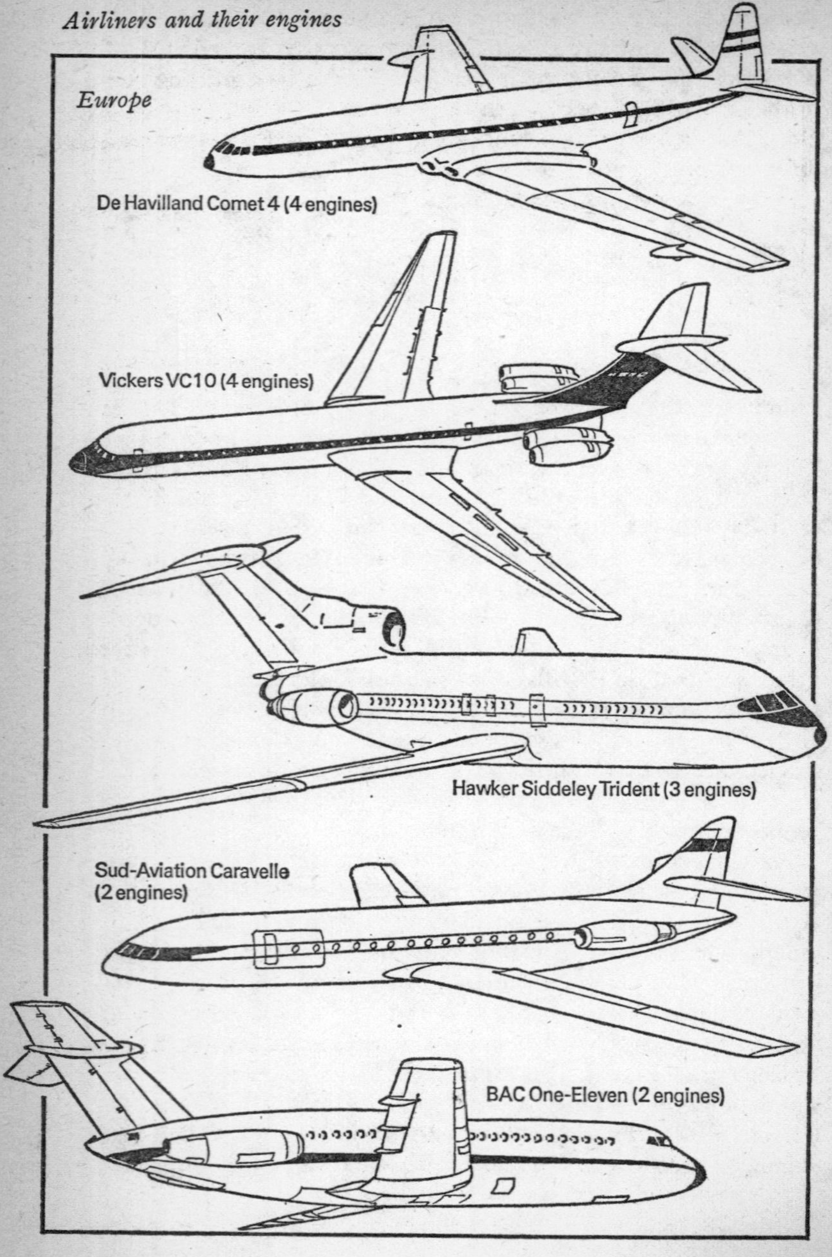
Europe
De Havilland Comet 4 (4 engines)
Vickers VC10 (4 engines)
Hawker Siddeley Trident (3 engines)
Sud-Aviation Caravelle
(2 engines)
BAC One-Eleven (2 engines)

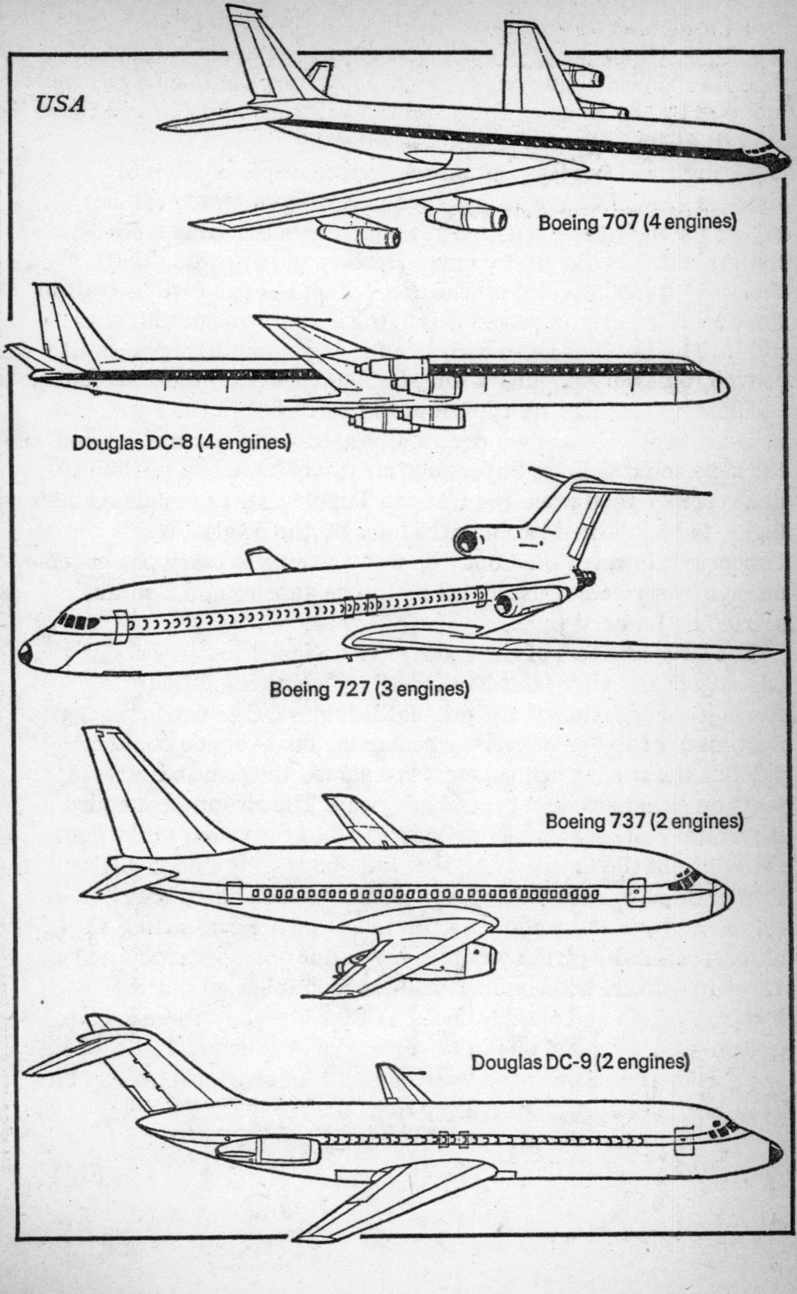
USA
Boeing 707 (4 engines)
Douglas DC-8 (4 engines)
Boeing 727 (3 engines)
Boeing 737 (2 engines)
Douglas DC-9 (2 engines)

Vickers built the four-engined VC 10 with two engines on each side of the rear fuselage. In all these European designs the wings were free of protruding engines but in America the Boeing 707 was followed by the Douglas DC-8 and Convairs 880 and 990 and these aircraft all had four engines on the wings.

Boeing and Douglas went on to produce whole families of airliners. Boeings have always favoured wing-mounted engines except for their three-engined 727 which uses the same layout as the Trident. The Boeing 727 made history in 1973 when the thousandth model rolled off the production line: no civil aircraft in the world had ever achieved this figure and orders continued to roll in. The Douglas DC-9 with two fuselage-mounted engines also proved to be very popular with sales figures around the 1000 mark.

These jet airliners are typical of the 1960s but in the 1970s two new dimensions in airliner design appeared – the 'Jumbo' jet and the supersonic airliner. Supersonic air travel became a possibility in December 1968 when the Russian Tupolev Tu-144 made its first flight, to be followed two months later by the Anglo-French Concorde. However the Concorde won the race to carry passengers on regular services when flights to Rio de Janeiro and Bahrain started in January 1976.

The large airliners of the 1960s were designed to carry about 180 passengers and were later 'stretched' by lengthening their fuselages. For instance, the original Douglas DC-8s carried a maximum of 173 passengers, whereas the final version could carry 257 but the seating arrangements remained the same with three seats on either side of a central gangway. The airlines demanded even larger airliners so the designers had to turn their attention to the width of the fuselage and the 'wide-body' jets emerged. The first of these was the Boeing 747 'Jumbo' which entered airline service in 1970 and could carry up to 490 passengers sitting 14 abreast. Like the earlier 707, the 747 had four engines mounted on the wings. Rival wide-bodied airliners soon followed but the Douglas DC-10 and the Lockheed TriStar both had three engines, one on each wing and one in the lower part of the fin. In Europe the Airbus Industrie A-300 was produced for shorter routes and it used just two wing-mounted engines.

Pilots and crews

Airliners have replaced ocean liners on almost all the routes linking the continents of the world yet they have retained many of the old nautical traditions and titles. An airliner is commanded by a Captain who is the senior pilot and the co-pilot is called the First Officer. Their cockpit is referred to as the *flight deck* while the passengers are housed in a *cabin*. Other members of the crew include Stewards and Stewardesses who look after the passengers and serve food from the *galleys*. On long-distance flights the crew may also include an Engineer, a Navigating Officer or a Radio Officer. As modern radio equipment is extremely reliable and simple to operate, the pilots usually cope without a Radio Officer. Navigating Officers too are becoming redundant as electronic equipment and computers take over. The Flight Engineer supervises a large instrument panel and his main responsibility is to ensure that the engines are running smoothly and using the correct amount of fuel. He must also ensure that the fuel is taken from the correct tanks otherwise the balance of the airliner could be upset.

All these crew members receive special training but none more so than the pilots. It takes many years of training and a considerable sum of money to produce an airline Captain. First he has to pass a selection board which includes a very tough medical examination: then he has to learn to fly. Student pilots are sent to special schools where they spend much of their time in the classroom learning about the principles of flight, aircraft construction, engines, instruments, systems, meteorology, air traffic control and aviation law. Of course the students are taught to fly: at first they are taken up by an instructor, then after ten to fifteen hours the student flies solo for the first time. But this is only the beginning, the next stage is a Private Pilot's Licence (PPL) and then after about two years' work the student obtains his Commercial Pilot's Licence (CPL). Even this is not the end of the line, for he has to learn how to fly the particular type of airliner his airline is operating – this is called a *rating*. Then the new pilot will probably fly as a spare third pilot for a while before he becomes a First Officer and it will be several years before he becomes a Captain.

Training the other crew members may not take such a long time

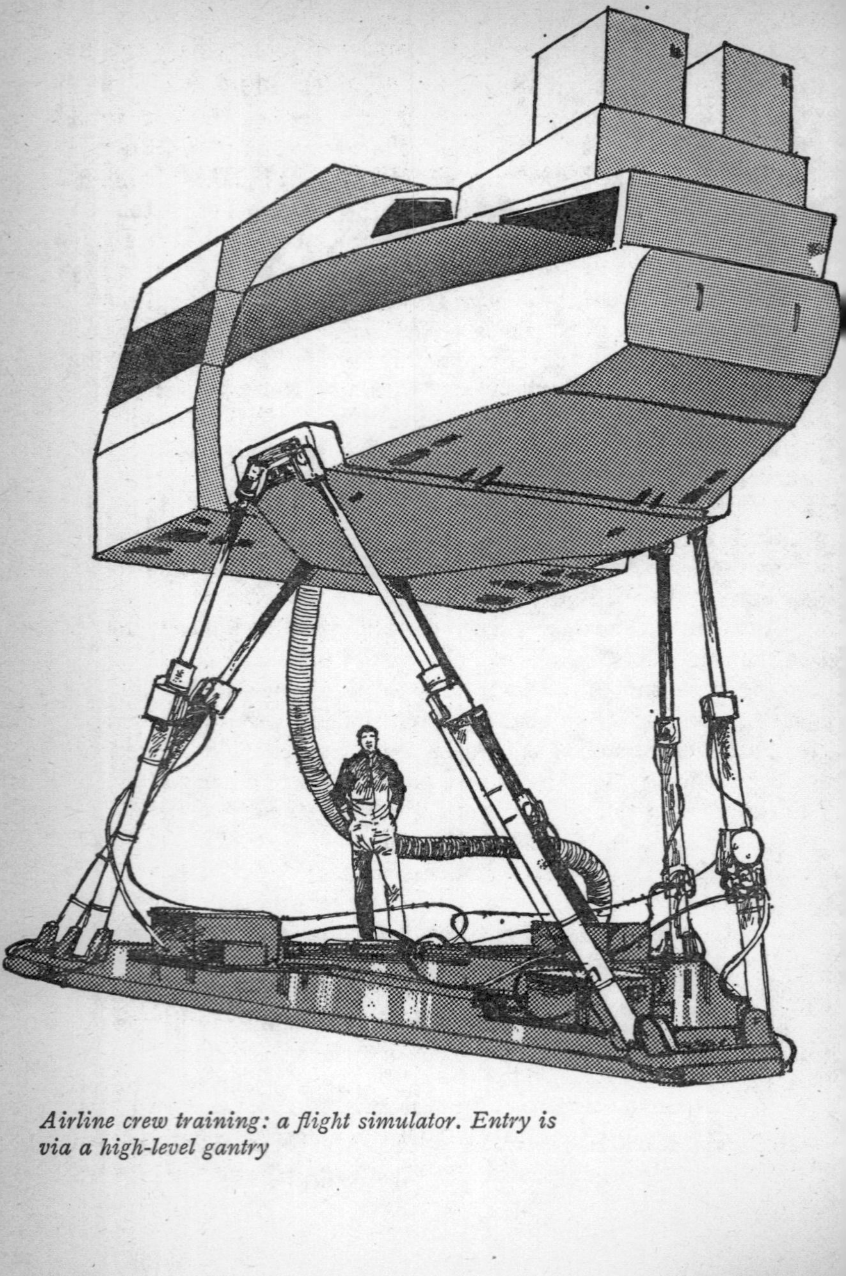

Airline crew training: a flight simulator. Entry is via a high-level gantry

but it is still vitally important. When everything is going according to plan their work is relatively straightforward but the whole crew must be ready for any emergency and know all the correct procedures. So a Stewardess learns how to serve coffee, but she must also know how to deal with frightened passengers should the airliner have to make a forced landing in the sea.

Airlines

There are about 500 airlines in the world and this figure does not include companies which fly only small aircraft. Of course some of the 500 have small fleets, for instance the French airline Air Fret has just one Boeing 707 and a staff of twenty employees – but this small airline has been flying since 1964. At the other extreme is the Russian airline Aeroflot with about 500,000 workers and an aircraft fleet of thousands. It is a little unfair to compare Aeroflot with other airlines because it is really a government department responsible for virtually all civilian aviation in the USSR. They carry passengers and cargo like any other airline but they also operate agricultural and ambulance aircraft and carry out fishery, ice and fire patrols.

The largest privately owned airline in the world is United Airlines of the United States, with a fleet of 360 aircraft and a staff of almost 50,000. The history of United Airlines goes back to 1931 when four pioneer airlines joined together, one of these, Varney Air Lines, having been founded in 1926. Today, United Airlines operate a large network of routes inside the United States and a few overseas services. United's foremost rivals within the United States are Eastern Air Lines, who introduced the *shuttle* service idea, and American Airlines who, over the years, have sponsored many new designs such as the Douglas DC-3 of 1936. The two major airlines of the United States flying on international routes are Pan American World Airways and Trans World Airlines. 'Pan Am' operate a round-the-world service and fly to most capital cities in the world.

In Europe the largest airlines are British Airways, Air France and Lufthansa German Airlines. Of these, British Airways is the largest company with a staff of over 50,000 and a fleet of over 200 aircraft. An unusual feature of this fleet is the fact that it consists of twenty-two different types of aircraft ranging from Concorde to small helicopters. Of course, until 1972 Britain had two national airlines: British Overseas Airways Corporation, which flew on the long-distance routes, and British European Airways, which operated services within Britain and to Europe. When these two airlines were joined together, two separate and very different fleets were combined into one which explains the high figure of twenty-two different types of aircraft. British Airways has the largest network of routes in the world covering 800,000 km (500,000 miles) and serving seventy-seven countries.

Airports

In the early days of aviation, aeroplanes could fly from any large field and these fields became known as *flight grounds* or *flying-grounds*. Gradually aircraft hangars and buildings for people were added and the name *aerodrome* was used. In the 1920s some of the larger civil aerodromes were called *airports* for the first time but smaller civil aircraft continued to operate from fields often called *landing-grounds* or *airstrips*. Military aerodromes were usually called *stations*, *air bases* or *airfields* but sometimes 'airfield' is used to describe the part of an airport used by the aircraft for take-off and landing.

In 1920 London's first real airport was opened at Croydon and like all airports it had grass runways. A great step forward was made in 1928 when New York's first airport was opened at Newark, for it had a hard-surfaced runway. Croydon remained a grass airfield until it was closed in 1959. During the Second World War many of the fighter bases were just grass airfields but the heavy bombers and transport aircraft needed hard-surfaced runways and some of these airfields were converted to airports after the war.

Today's airports have come a long way from the early days of Newark and Croydon when passengers were measured in thousands. John F. Kennedy Airport, New York, and London Heathrow handle many millions of passengers every year and they never stop expanding. In fact a large modern airport can be compared with a town with a working population of 50,000 or more. There are shops,

The RAF's Red Arrows team (*see page* 127)

Airports old and new. Croydon as it was in the 1920s *(above) and Dulles, Washington (top), today.*

banks, restaurants, bars, hotels, buses, taxis, cars and car parks. In addition there are all the workers who ensure that everything runs smoothly – telephone operators, receptionists, police, firemen, electricians and cleaners. All these services and people could be found in any town but at the airport there are also many staff working for the airlines. Some of these look after passengers on the ground and in the air, while others service the aircraft between flights and overhaul them at regular intervals.

Building a new airport presents many problems for the surveyors, engineers and meteorologists looking for a perfect site. If the airport is to serve a city it must be near the city centre, but on the other hand the noise of its aircraft should not disturb the residents. Runways have to be built on solid ground to withstand the landing impact of large airliners and they cover a large area, consequently the only available site is usually miles out of the city. The ends of the runways must be free of dangerous obstructions such as tall buildings and hills. Weather conditions too have to be studied to ensure that the area is not prone to mist and fog but there should be an alternative airport somewhere near – just in case.

Aircraft servicing

A motor car runs more efficiently and reliably if it is serviced regularly. It needs petrol and oil every few days, tyres have to be checked, cleaning is necessary, at regular intervals it goes into a garage for a service and, if it is over three years old, once a year it has to be tested by a Government-approved test centre. With aircraft it is even more important that they are reliable. If a car breaks down it can pull into the kerb – which might be inconvenient – but if an airliner breaks down when flying high in the sky it could be a major disaster.

When an airliner lands after a flight it is immediately surrounded by a fleet of vehicles of all shapes and sizes. One of the first to arrive is a mobile power unit which supplies electricity to the stationary aircraft. Then there is the air-conditioning truck with an engine-driven air compressor which pumps air into the passenger cabin to keep it at a comfortable temperature. Sometimes fuel is brought to the aircraft in tankers but at many modern airports

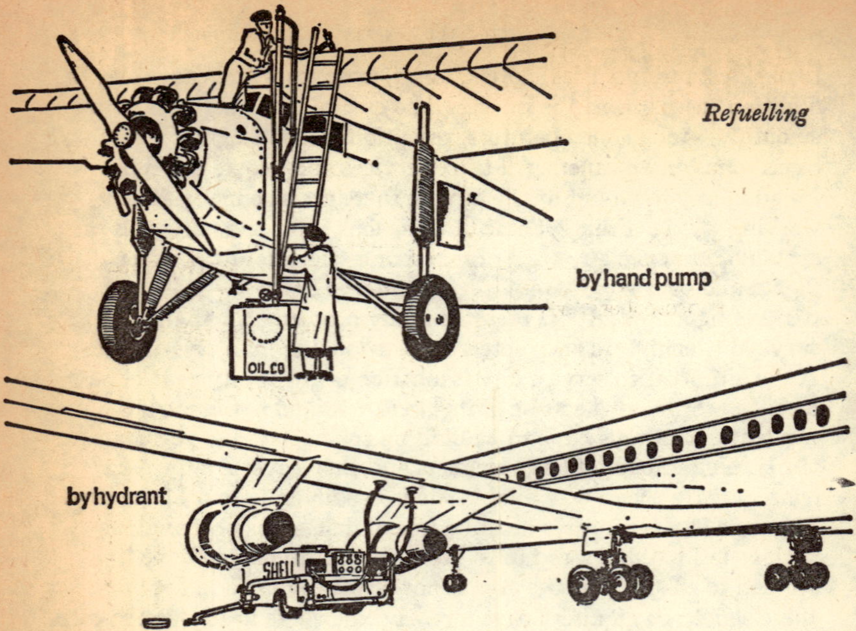

Refuelling

fuel is piped to the serving areas and a hose connects the aircraft to a *hydrant*. Fuel is pumped aboard at very high speed – it would fill a motor car's petrol tank in a fraction of a second. Oil and water are both brought to the aircraft in small tankers. Engineers give the aircraft a routine between-flights inspection to make sure that there are no loose parts or fuel leaks. Other vehicles are busy looking after the passenger's requirements – transporting baggage, removing rubbish, bringing fresh food and drink and emptying the toilets.

Every few weeks the aircraft is taken out of service for a minor overhaul, then there are graded checks up to a major overhaul which involves stripping down the aircraft to inspect every component. Naturally this takes a long time but it only has to be done every few years. By careful planning the airlines try to arrange for these overhauls to be carried out in the winter months.

Before any aircraft can fly it must have a *Certificate of Airworthiness* and this is issued by a Government Department. In Britain inspectors of the Civil Aviation Authority ensure that aircraft meet the very high standards of safety demanded before issuing a 'C of A'.

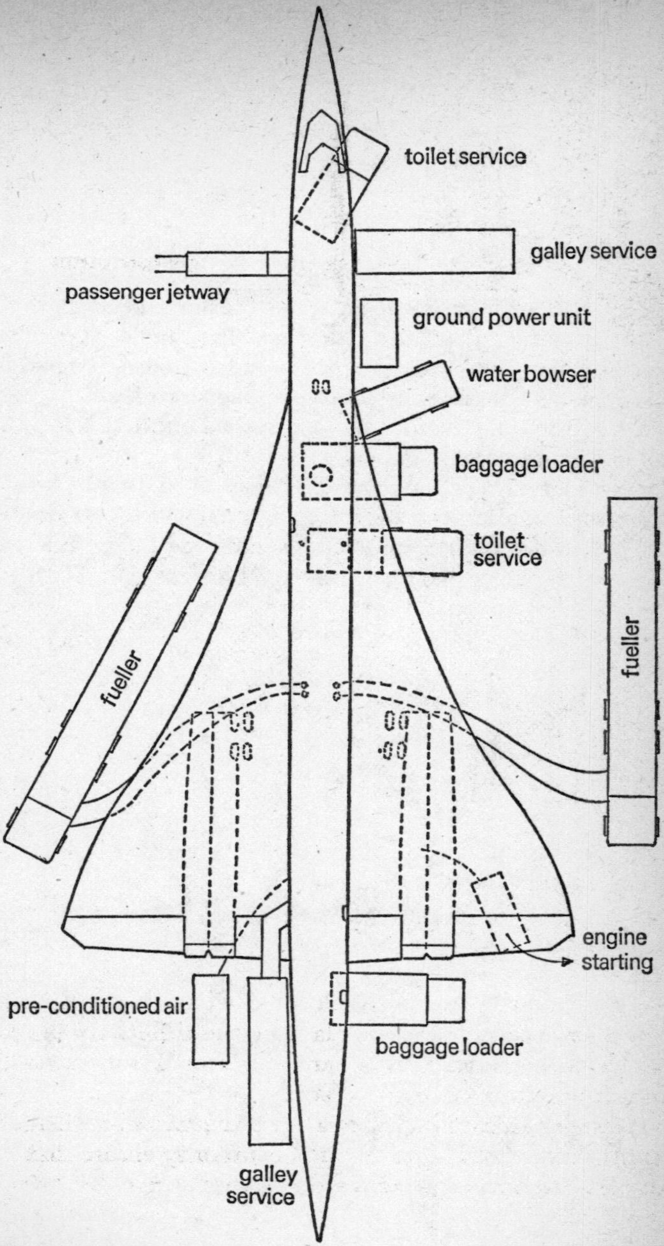

Aircraft servicing: Concorde

Navigation

In the early days of aviation, pilots found their way by map-reading with the help of a compass. Railway lines and rivers were a great help – in fact some railways stations had their names painted on the roof to help pilots. When oceans had to be crossed there were no such landmarks for the pilot to *fix* his position but a compass course needed to be checked so the airmen copied the sailors and used a *sextant*. This instrument measures the angle between the horizon and the sun, moon or a star: from these angles and a book of tables, the navigator's position can be calculated. Of course this operation takes some time and a fast-moving aircraft will have moved on by the time the fix has been worked out, but this method is still used occasionally.

Between the two World Wars radio began to be used to assist the navigator. An aircraft transmitted a signal which two ground stations picked up on *direction-finding* aerials and these gave two *bearings* which enabled the navigator to fix his position. During the

Navigation: using a sextant to measure the inclination of the sun or a star. An aircraft navigator uses a sextant with a bubble (spirit level) instead of sighting the horizon.

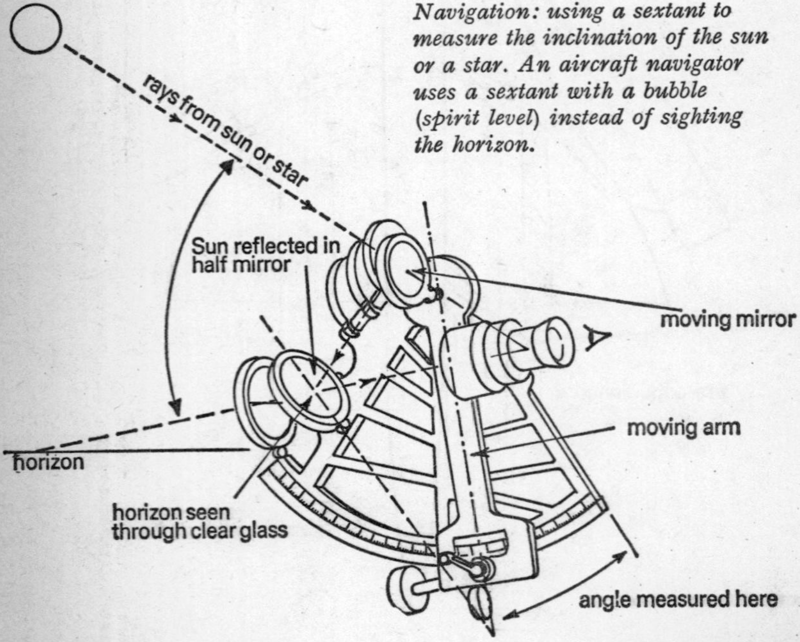

Second World War new radio aids to navigation were invented to help bombers find their targets over enemy territory – where there were no helpful direction-finding ground stations. The very successful British Systems were called *Gee* and *Loran*. From these the *Decca Navigator* was developed which could show the aircraft's position on a moving map. In the United States another system was developed called *VOR/DME* (Very-high-frequency Omni-directional Radio-range/Distance Measuring Equipment). This could be described as a lighthouse sending out radio signals instead of light. An instrument in the aircraft picked up these signals and worked out a fix. Both the Decca system and VOR/DME needed ground stations so for long distance flights over the sea some other system was needed. First came *Doppler* which used radar mounted in the aircraft to measure its track and speed, then the *Inertial Navigation System* which is also used to navigate in outer space. This very complicated system uses gyroscopes, acceleration-measuring instruments and computers.

Aerial navigation: using direction-finding aerials.

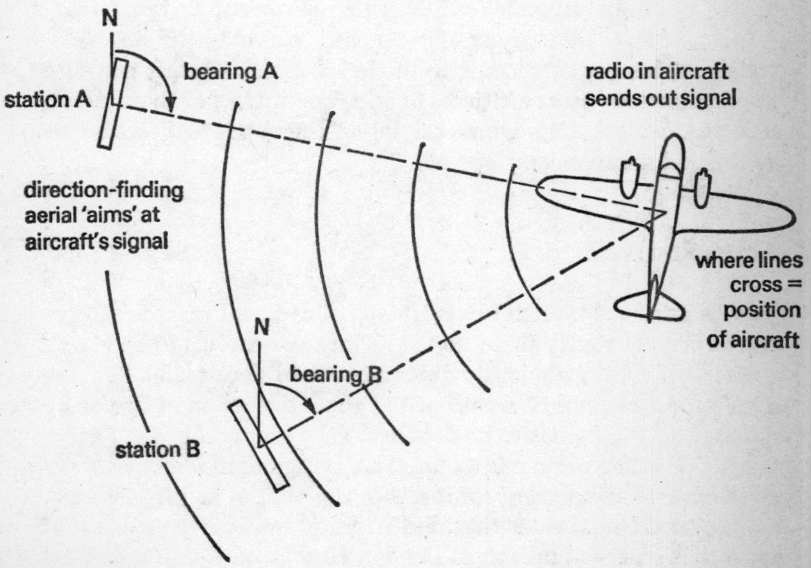

Airways

As more and more airliners were built in the 1920s it became clear that they had to be controlled in some way – especially over the busy regions such as the United States and Europe. *Airways* were introduced as the 'highways of the air' to keep the airliners from getting lost or colliding with each other. A radio beam was transmitted from a *radio-range* station and aimed along an airway. Following this beam was so simple that the pilots could navigate without the aid of a navigator. They just listened to the signal from the range on their headphones and when they heard a steady note the aircraft was on course. To obtain a fix the pilot tuned in to a *fan-marker* beacon which transmitted a signal upwards. A receiver in the aircraft picked up this signal only when the aircraft was passing over the beacon. The old radio beacons have now been superseded by the modern systems of radio navigation – primarily VOR/DME.

Most of the world's major airports are now linked by airways which are controlled internationally and identified by numbers. In some ways they resemble roads but there is one important difference, they have height. This is used to avoid head-on collisions: instead of keeping to the left or right, aircraft travelling in one direction fly at altitudes of an even number of thousands of feet (e.g. 28,000), then aircraft flying in the opposite direction keep to the odd numbers (e.g. 27,000).

Air traffic control

Just as any road system needs traffic police to enforce the safety rules of the Highway Code, so the airway system has to be controlled. This is obviously quite a problem since traffic lights or a policeman can not be positioned at the intersection of two airways. All the controlling has to be done from the ground by *Air Traffic Controllers* using radio and radar. This is organised in stages depending on conditions, for instance the pilot of an airliner on a transatlantic flight finds that mid-Atlantic traffic is very different from that on the approach to London Heathrow. Large areas, such

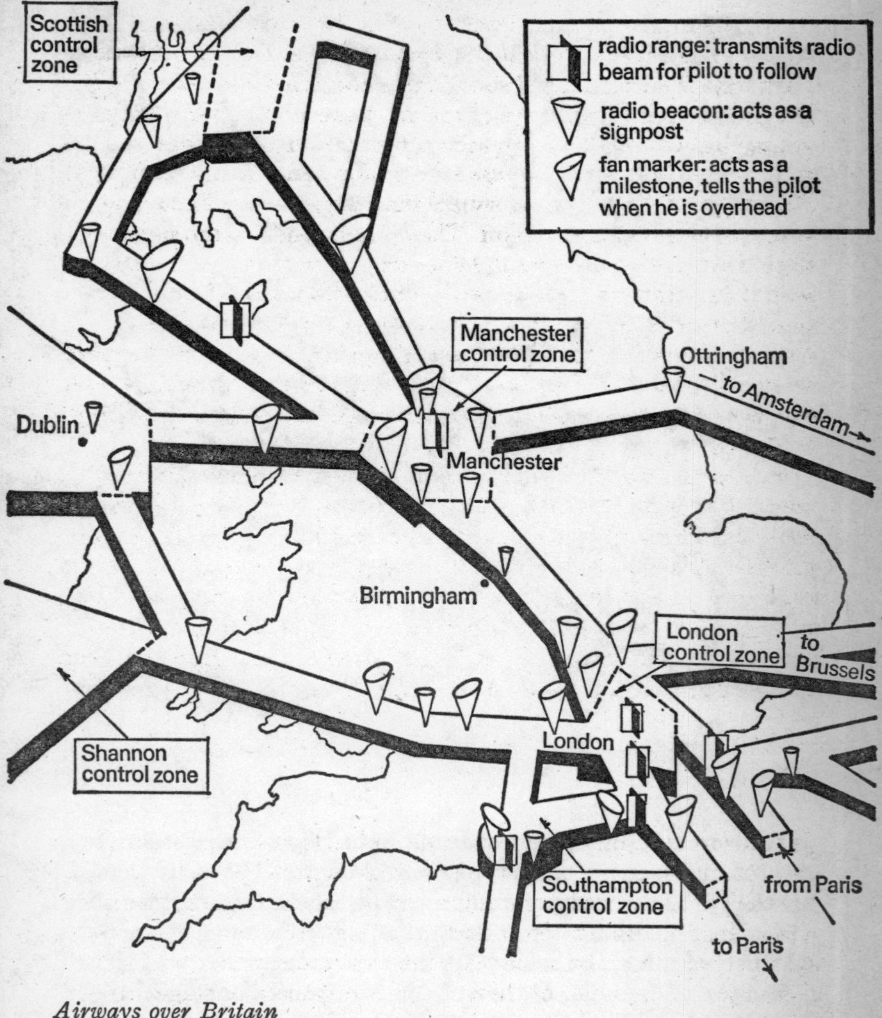

Airways over Britain

Controllers at the London Air Traffic Control Centre

as the North Atlantic, are divided up into *Flight Information Regions* and each region has one Control Centre. The controllers tell the pilot at what height and speed he should fly, and then they ensure that no other aircraft fly at that height unless they are a safe distance ahead or behind. As the airliner nears Britain it is picked up by the radar of the London Air Traffic Control Centre at West Drayton, Middlesex. The controllers of this busy centre use a very advanced computer system called *Mediator* which is linked to three radar sites. The radar scanners track each aircraft in the area and the computer predicts their flight path. To do this the computer has to store a host of information such as details of each aircraft's performance, the weather forecast and airway rules and regulations. With Mediator the controllers guide each airliner to within 20 km (12 miles) of Heathrow. At this point the airliner is handed over to the *Approach Controllers* who are based in a darkened room crowded with radar screens. Their job is to maintain a steady flow of aircraft to or from the runways. The final stages of a landing are controlled from the glass-house on the top of the control tower by the *Air Controllers*. After landing, the *Ground Controllers* direct the airliner to its parking area.

Landing in poor visibility is probably the most dangerous part of flying but with the help of modern radio and radar aids the risks can be reduced. For many years pilots have been able to use an *Instrument Landing System* (ILS) which could guide them almost on to the runway, or the Approach Controller could 'talk him down' using radar. More recently however, improved systems are being introduced including automatic landing equipment which can land an airliner without any assistance from the pilot.

International control

Because so many airliner flights involve flying to more than one country, an international body was set up to ensure that all airlines and Air Traffic Controllers have a standard way of working. The International Civil Aviation Organisation (ICAO) was founded as an offshoot of the United Nations and today about 150 countries are members. After detailed research and discussion ICAO make their recommendations and it is then up to the member nations to enforce these agreed standards. For instance, it is vitally important that all aircraft observe the same rules of the air and procedures, especially when approaching an airport. To avoid language problems, English was chosen as the international language for controllers and pilots, and a phonetic alphabet was introduced: A for Alpha, B for Bravo, etc. Other items covered include such things as maps, radio and navigational aids, aircraft inspection and even licences for personnel.

Being a body representing governments, ICAO can deal directly with such items as frontier restrictions which involve considerable paper work and delay on the ground. This international red tape has been drastically reduced. ICAO also persuades governments to keep their navigational aids, weather forecasting services and airports up to the required standard. If a country cannot afford to do this, financial help may be given.

There is a second international organisation influencing air travel but unlike ICAO it is made up of the airlines themselves and is called the International Air Transport Association (IATA). IATA was founded as long ago as 1919 but for many years it was little more than an association of European airlines. The world-wide organisation which exists today has been operating since 1945. The work of IATA which affects the traveller most directly is reflected in the airline ticket. Fares are agreed between the IATA members and this eliminates competition which might lead to tempting fare reductions paid for by cutting down on aircraft maintenance. Also, every airline ticket office of an IATA member sells tickets for all the other members. Sometimes a journey may involve two or more flights on different airlines but this is no problem – one ticket is sufficient. This interchangeable ticket is very convenient for the air traveller but requires much work behind the scenes to ensure that the airline which carries the passenger gets the money. The IATA *clearing house* staff work out how much money is due to each member airline. Many other financial, commercial and technical problems are solved by the joint efforts of the airlines through IATA.

Freight by air

In the 1930s a few sacks of airmail letters carried on a passenger service represented a typical load of aerial freight. Today the picture has changed dramatically, and is still changing for each year both the quantity and the variety of goods carried by air increases. Mail is still carried, but so too are orchids, elephants, ship's propellers, gas cookers, racing cars, gold bullion and newspapers. Even a pig can fly as Lord Brabazon proved back in 1908 when he took a piglet for a short flip – just to disprove the old saying. From this light-hearted beginning has grown an important part of the air freight business – the transporting of animals. It has

Carvair car ferry

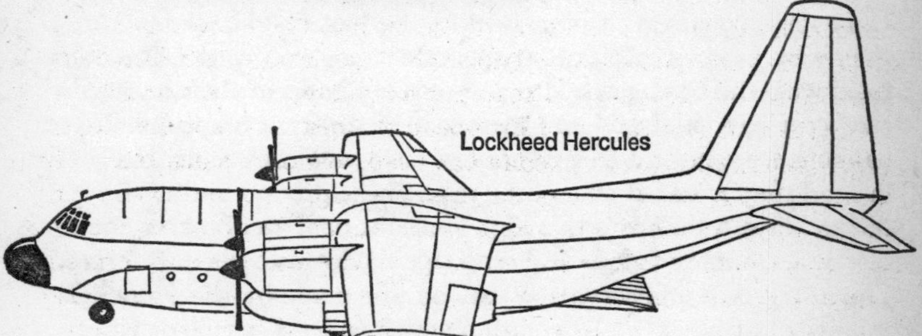

Lockheed Hercules

Air freighters

even been claimed that every fourth passenger carried by one airline is an animal, a fish, a bird or a reptile.

Aircraft adapted to transport freight were first used on a large scale during the Second World War. Many of these military freighters were converted from airliners by removing the seats, and incorporating a large loading door and a reinforced floor. After the war several airlines started flying items of freight, on a small scale, using these old military freighters. So freight services were gradually built up by the Cinderellas of the airlines' fleet. Today however the boom in freight by air calls for specially designed aircraft such as the Lockheed Hercules with its extra-large doors, huge fuselage and load capacity of over 20,000 kg (20 tons). Even passenger aircraft are expected to carry a considerable load of freight in holds below the cabin floor – in addition to a load of passengers.

The cost of transporting anything by aircraft is greater than by lorry, train or ship but even so freight by air is expanding. There are three main reasons for the aircraft's increasing popularity: it is very much faster than any of its rivals, inaccessible regions can be reached by air when all else fails, and finally, fragile goods can be carried by air with far less risk of damage.

4 Military Aircraft

Aerial observation posts: balloons and scouts

Only eleven years after man-carrying balloons had been invented, they were pressed into military service as look-out posts. Balloons filled with the light gas hydrogen were used and in their baskets they carried a pilot and an observer armed with a telescope. These balloons were not set free, otherwise they would have drifted away: instead they were attached by a rope to the ground and flown rather like a kite. From this high look-out post an observer could spy on the enemy troops and send signals down to his own forces. The first military observation balloon was made by the French in 1794, shortly after the Revolution which ended the rule of King Louis XVI. It was tried out at the town of Maubeuge to observe enemy troops from Austria and Holland who were positioned just outside the town. But this particular balloon had an even greater triumph a few weeks later on 26th June 1794, at the Battle of Fleurus. A French General ascended in the balloon and for about ten hours he directed operations from above. Written messages were lowered down or hauled up by the high-flying General. But the presence of the balloon had another effect on the battle, as most of the Austrian troops had never seen a balloon before and a rumour spread that the French were in league with the devil. The Austrians were thoroughly disheartened and the French won a great victory – the first battle in which air power played an important part.

History has a strange way of repeating itself and this is what happened when the aeroplane was invented. Eleven years after the Wright brothers' first flight, the First World War broke out and aeroplanes became look-out posts for the armies – like the balloon 120 years earlier. Of course aircraft had several advantages over balloons because they could fly right over the enemy lines and they were much more difficult to shoot down from the ground. Observation balloons were still used, but they had to be kept some way back from the front lines and the dangers of enemy gun-fire. The army commanders had two tasks to be carried out in the air.

Observation balloon at the Battle of Fleurus, 1794

BE2c

One was 'spotting' for their guns. This meant observing where the shells were landing and then signalling instructions to the gunners which helped them to hit their targets. Balloons were used for this work together with slow *reconnaissance* aircraft such as the two-seater B.E.2c designed at the Royal Aircraft Factory, Farnborough. The army's other job for aeroplanes was to make reconnaissance flights behind the enemy lines to see what the opposing troops were doing. Faster aircraft were used for this work and they were called *scouts* as the army commanders thought of them as an aerial version of the old cavalry scout. Guns were not fitted to any of these aircraft for the authorities had said there was 'no great likelihood of aerial scouts coming into conflict' – how wrong they were!

Fighters

Britain had two very useful fast single-seater scouts in service with the Royal Flying Corps during 1914; the Bristol Scout and the Sopwith Tabloid. Both were small biplanes capable of about 160 km/h (100 mph) (and the Tabloid had already made a name for itself by winning the second Schneider Trophy race just before the war started) but neither aircraft was armed although the pilots usually carried a rifle or revolver with them just in case they met an enemy scout.

A new era of aerial warfare began on 1st April 1915 when a French pilot took off in his Morane-Saulnier Type L scout. The

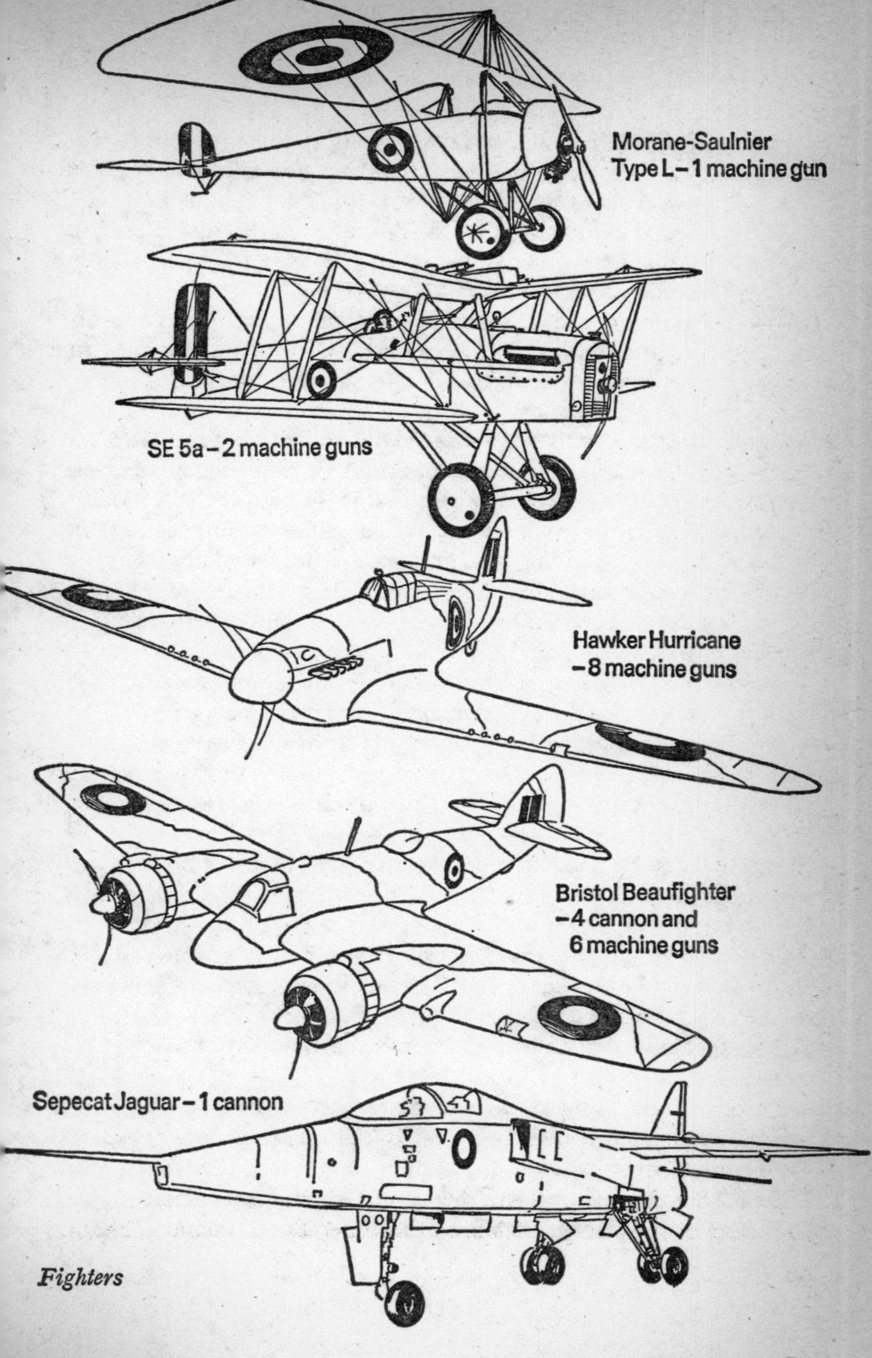
Morane-Saulnier
Type L – 1 machine gun
SE 5a – 2 machine guns
Hawker Hurricane
– 8 machine guns
Bristol Beaufighter
– 4 cannon and
6 machine guns
Sepecat Jaguar – 1 cannon

Fighters

pilot, called Roland Garros, had fitted a machine gun to the nose of his aircraft just in front of the cockpit so that the gun could fire forwards. This enabled him to aim the gun by flying his aircraft straight towards the enemy. Of course the problem was to prevent the bullets from shooting away his own propeller and he did this by bolting small steel wedges to the propeller blades just in line with the barrel of the gun. These wedges protected the propeller by deflecting away any bullets which did happen to hit it. German engineers and the Dutch aircraft designer Anthony Fokker went a stage further and produced an aeroplane fitted with a forward-firing machine gun which did not need dangerous deflector plates. The mechanism which actually fired the bullets was connected to the engine in such a way that it operated only when the propeller blades were not in the direct line of fire. A Fokker monoplane was fitted with this new *interrupter gear* and in July 1915 the 'Fokker Scourge' began. The combination of this manoeuvrable monoplane with its forward-firing machine gun made it far superior to any other fighting aircraft. British and French machines were hopelessly outclassed and for several months the Germans ruled the air.

By 1916 the British and French had developed interrupter gears so they were able to fit forward-firing machine guns to aeroplanes with a propeller at the front. Both sides were now building aircraft specifically designed to fight: the fighter aircraft had emerged from the scout, but the old name stuck for some time. Monoplanes, biplanes and triplanes were tried, as were single- or two-seaters. By the end of the war the single-seater biplane with two machine guns firing through the propeller emerged as the most successful fighter layout and remained so until the Second World War. One such biplane was the sleek Hawker Fury which was Britain's number one fighter until 1938. Another biplane fighter was still in service with the RAF when the war started – the Gloster Gladiator which had an increased armament of four machine guns.

During the 1930s forward-looking designers were at last making a break from the old two-gun biplane layout and proposing monoplanes armed with eight machine guns. From the Hawker Fury a 'Monoplane Fury' was developed which became better known as the Hurricane, and from the Supermarine racing seaplanes, built for the Schneider Trophy races, came the Spitfire. Both the Hurricane and Spitfire made a name for themselves during the Battle of Britain in 1940 when their rival fighters were the Messerschmitt Bf109 and the twin-engined Bf110. These German fighters were armed with cannon in addition to machine guns: a machine gun fires solid bullets but a cannon fires explosive shells. During the war a mixture of cannon and machine guns was the usual fighter armament: the Bristol Beaufighter with four cannon and six machine guns was one of the most heavily armed.

As the Second World War drew to a close, jet and rocket fighters joined the older piston-engined machines. Rocket-projectiles were being carried in addition to guns and bombs, for fighters had become fighter-bombers, and were being used to attack ground targets. In the years after the war, supersonic fighters were introduced: the first to enter service was the North American F-100A Super Sabre. Today's fighters are usually multi-purpose aircraft, like the old fighter-bombers, and include the Anglo-French Jaguar, the European Panavia Tornado, the American McDonnell Douglas F-15 Eagle and the Russian Mikoyan MIG-25 (Foxbat). This new generation of fighter carries not only high-powered cannon but also *air-to-air* guided missiles. These rocket-propelled missiles are either guided to the target aircraft by radar or they seek out the target for themselves by following the *infra-red* heat from its jet engine. The American Sparrow uses radar while their Sidewinder and the British Firestreak have an infra-red heat seeker.

Bombers and bombs

The idea of dropping bombs from the air goes back to the days of the balloon, for in 1849 Venice was bombed. The Austrians were besieging Venice and they made some 200 small hot-air balloons each carrying a 12-kilogram bomb which could be dropped by a time fuse. When the wind was blowing in the right direction the balloons were released, but the raid was not a great success. A few bombs reached their target and did little damage, while others drifted back and landed on the senders! Probably the first bombs to be dropped from an aeroplane were those dropped in 1911 by an Italian aircraft during fighting in North Africa.

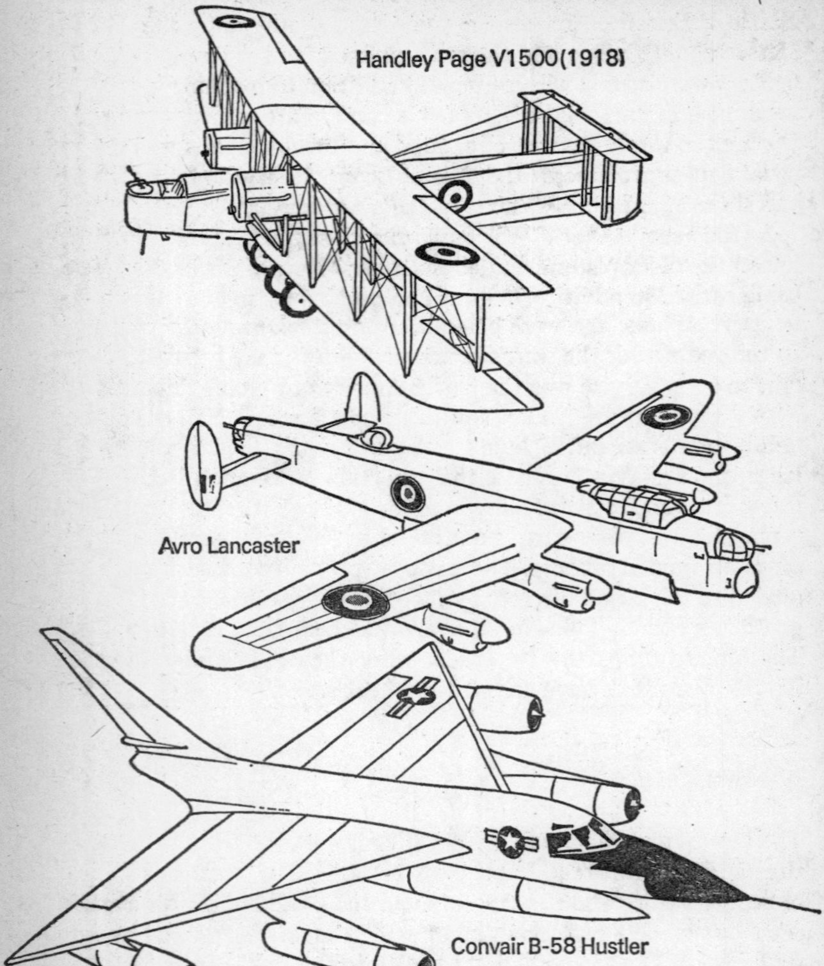
Handley Page V1500(1918)
Avro Lancaster
Convair B-58 Hustler

Bombers

When the First World War broke out in 1914 bombing raids were carried out within a few days. French Voisin IIIs and British Avro 504s attacked Zeppelin bases in Germany but the bombs were very small and did little damage. However, in Russia a new era in bombers had begun in January 1914 when Igor Sikorsky flew the first ever four-engined bomber which he called Ilya Mourometz. About eighty similar aircraft were built and used by the Russians. In Europe two different types of bomber were produced: fast, light day-bombers such as the de Havilland D.H.9A, and heavy night bombers such as the German Gotha G.V. and the British Handley Page 0/100, 0/400 and V/1500. The V/1500 could carry two 1500 kg bombs compared with the 10 kg bombs used early in the war.

Between the wars there was very little change in bomber design: the light day bomber was still the mainstay of most airforces. In Britain the Hawker Hart two-seater biplane was outstanding as it was faster than most fighter aircraft. Then in the late 1930s monoplane bombers began to appear, also a new breed of light bomber designed for dive-bombing, such as the notorious Junkers Ju 87 Stuka. The backbone of most bomber forces, however, was the twin-engined monoplane of which the Vickers Wellington and the German Heinkel He 111 were excellent examples as they remained in service throughout the war in various roles.

During the Second World War a new generation of four-engined heavy bombers came into service with the RAF's Short Stirling, Handley Page Halifax and Avro Lancaster. These bombers usually flew at night, while the United States Air Force flew daylight missions with the Boeing B-17 Flying Fortress and Consolidated B-24 Liberator. Bomb loads increased dramatically during the war, for example the Heinkel He 111 could carry about 2000 kg of bombs whereas a Lancaster could carry a single ten-ton bomb (10,000 kg). Incidentally, this huge bomb was called a 'Grand Slam' and it was designed by Barnes Wallis who also designed the bouncing bomb used in the famous dam-busting raid of 1943. Despite these large bombers, the fast, light bomber still had an important part to play and one of the most successful was the de Havilland Mosquito. Like its predecessor the Hawker Hart, it was faster than most fighters yet it could carry 1800 kg of bombs. Towards the end of the war the Germans introduced two new light bombers, the Messerschmitt Me262 and the Arado Ar234B Blitz which were both powered by jet engines. The war finally ended when two devastating atomic bombs were dropped on Japan by Boeing B-29 Superfortresses.

Since the Second World War many jet bombers have been built and the first generation were all subsonic. One of the most successful light bombers was the English Electric Canberra, while the heavyweights included the Avro Vulcan, the American Boeing B-47 Stratojet and the Boeing B-52 Stratofortress. Supersonic bombers were introduced in 1960 when the United States Air Force received its first Convair B-58 Hustler. This *delta-winged* aircraft could fly at twice the speed of sound (Mach 2) and carry a nuclear bomb. It has since been replaced by the swing-wing General Dynamics FB-111 which can fly at Mach 2.5. In addition to normal high speed missions, the FB-111 can fly subsonically at just 60 metres above the ground to avoid detection by the enemy radar. The aircraft is guided over the ground automatically by its own *terrain-following radar* – a far cry from the hot-air balloon bombs drifting in the wind.

Reconnaissance aircraft

The activities of the early scout aircraft in the First World War and how these so-called scouts became fighters have already been described. Observation aircraft were used to carry out reconnaissance flights but because these were slow and vulnerable to attack they had to be escorted by scouts (or fighters). One typical aircraft was the Royal Aircraft Factory B.E.2c which had a top speed of about 115 km/h (70 mph): nevertheless it was a very steady flier and this made it ideal for aerial photography. Observers could not remember all the things they saw on a long mission, so cameras were carried to bring back a permanent record.

Reconnaissance aircraft of a very different kind were also used during the First World War: airships patrolled the seas looking out for enemy naval forces. Many British non-rigid airships carried out long and cold flights over the North Sea searching for the German Grand Fleet or lurking submarines. Immediately after the war there was very little need for reconnaissance aircraft but in the 1930s several were produced. The Avro Anson, with its

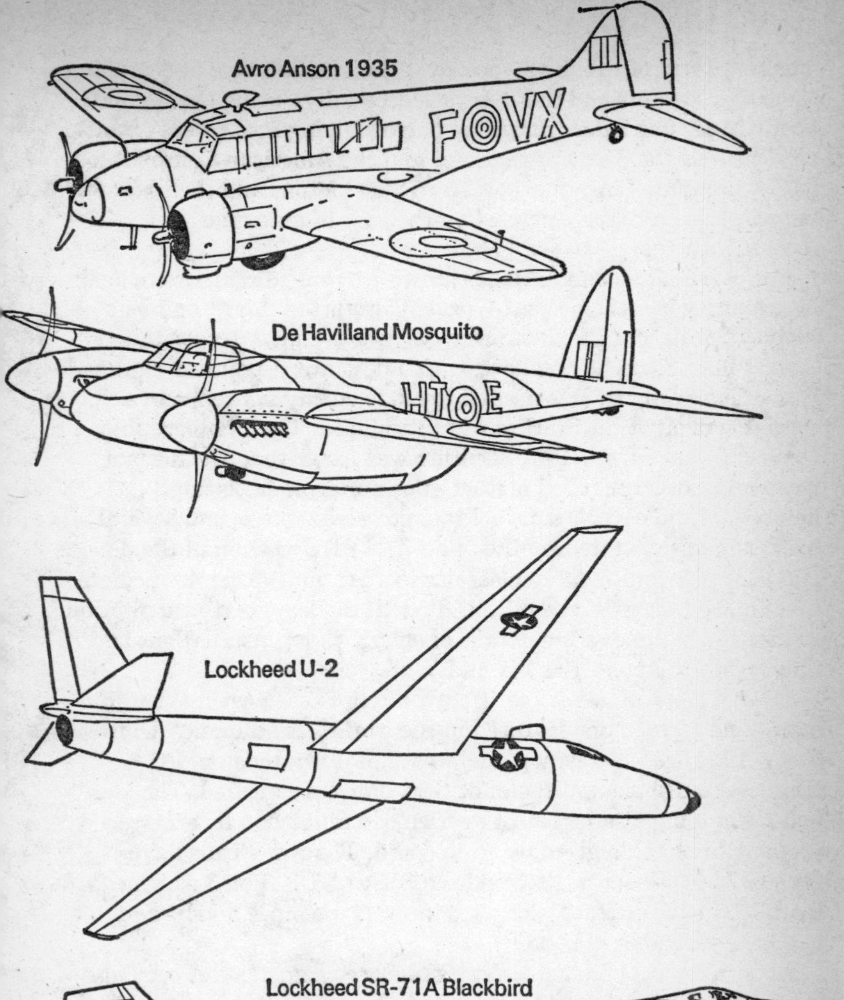

Reconnaissance aircraft

'conservatory' of windows, took over the airship's role of patrolling the coastal waters and did it very successfully during the Second World War. For longer maritime patrols, flying boats were often used such as the Short Sunderland and the American Consolidated PBY5 Catalina. Since the war, Avro Shackletons and then Hawker Siddeley Nimrods have carried on the task of maritime reconnaissance.

For overland reconnaissance camera-carrying aircraft were again in demand when the Second World War started. Light bombers such as the Bristol Blenheim were very convenient because the bomb-aimer could be equipped with a downward-pointing camera. But a faster aircraft was needed to elude enemy fighters and a special version of the Spitfire was introduced. The Photographic Reconnaissance Unit (PRU) Spitfire was faster than the normal version because it carried neither guns nor armour plating: however, it did carry extra fuel to increase its range, and several fixed cameras operated by the pilot. The PRU version of the de Havilland Mosquito entered service in 1941 and was an immediate success. The crews of these PRU aircraft made a great contribution to victory by discovering details of enemy radar installations and their secret weapons, the V-1 and V-2.

The use of reconnaissance aircraft did not cease when the war ended and in 1960 one featured in the world's headlines. A United States Lockheed U-2 'spy plane' was shot down by a guided missile over Russia and the pilot Gary Powers captured. The U-2 had been flying at a height of over 20,000 m (68,000 ft) and was thought to be too high to be intercepted. The Americans have replaced the U-2 with the Lockheed SR-71A Blackbird which can fly much faster at Mach 3 or 3700 km/h (2300 mph) and at a height of 24,400 m (80,000 ft).

Modern reconnaissance aircraft still carry cameras but they also carry some very ingenious equipment. Their cameras can 'see' in the dark: their sideways-looking radar records its 'sightings' on film and a device called an *infra-red linescan* measures heat and decides whether the engine of a parked aircraft has been run recently!

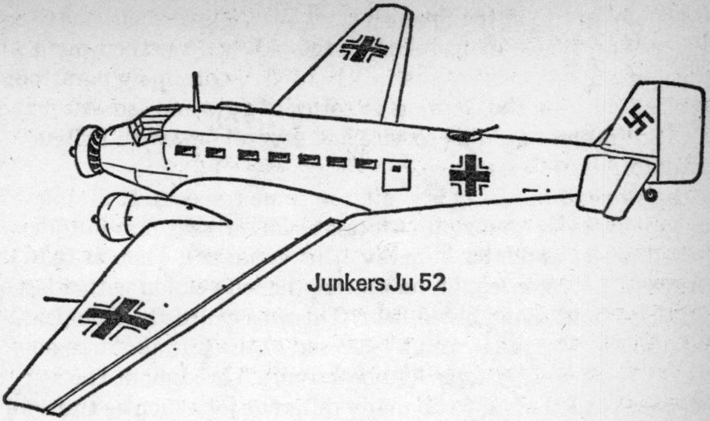

Junkers Ju 52

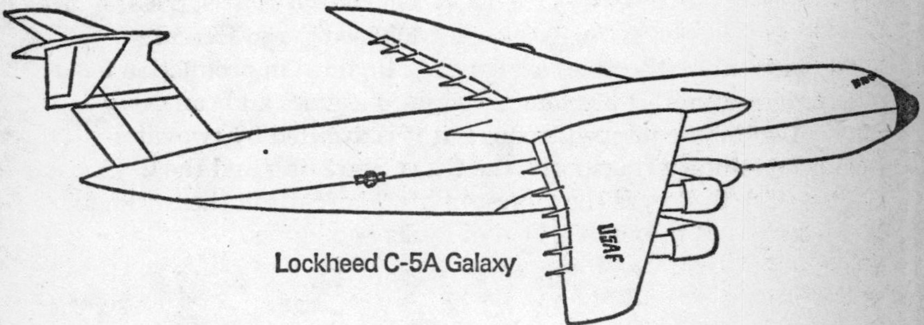

Lockheed C-5A Galaxy

Transport aircraft

Although a few First World War bombers were adapted to carry important equipment and passengers, real military transport aircraft were developed from civilian airliners of the 1930s. Two airliners in particular which played a vital part in this transformation were the German Junkers Ju 52/3m and the American Douglas DC-3. The Junkers Ju 52 was a three-engined (hence 3m) monoplane with a rather unusual corrugated skin. It first appeared in 1932 as an airliner but in 1936 it was converted into a bomber and troop transport for use in the Spanish Civil War. Throughout the Second World War the Germans relied on the old Ju 52 as their main transport aircraft and it was widely used for dropping paratroops especially during the German victories of 1939 and '40. After the war it returned to airline service and several flew with British European Airways.

The story of the DC-3 is similar in some respects. It first flew in 1935 and was an immediate success as an airliner, first in the United States and later in many other countries. Then in 1940 the Army Air Corps ordered a new strengthened version with a large cargo door and a reinforced floor. This was called the Douglas C-47, or Dakota in the RAF, and by the end of the war about 10,000 DC-3s, C-47s and Dakotas had been built. Throughout the war they were called upon to do many different jobs such as transporting troops and supplies, dropping paratroops and towing gliders. When the war ended many were converted back to airliners and even in the 1970s several hundred were still in service.

Other military transports followed but few equalled the versatility of the Ju 52 and the DC-3. One of the most successful in recent years has been the American Lockheed C-130 Hercules which first entered service in 1956 and remained in production for over twenty years. It has four turbo-prop engines and can carry ninety-two fully-equipped troops but it is dwarfed by two later Lockheed military transports, the C-141 StarLifter and the C-5A Galaxy. The Galaxy is the largest military aircraft in the world, for it can carry 345 troops or a load of tanks and lorries.

Naval aircraft

Naval aviation began in 1910–11 with several notable flights showing how aircraft could be adapted for use at sea. The first aeroplane to take-off from water was a strange-looking tail-first floatplane flown by a French pilot, Henri Fabre. The date was 28th March 1910. In the following year an American designer, Glenn Curtiss, built the first really practical seaplane and later an aeroplane which could fly from land or water – an *amphibian.* However, the naval experts wanted to carry their aircraft on board ships. This was quite possible but it took a long time to lower a

seaplane by crane from the deck to the water so they requested an aircraft which could take off from the deck of a ship. In 1910 the United States light cruiser *Birmingham* had a ramp measuring only 25m (82 ft) built on the forward part of the hull. The first aeroplane flight from a ship took place at Norfolk, Virginia on 14th November 1910 when a Curtiss Model D piloted by Eugene Ely struggled off this ramp. The Curtiss biplane fell and actually hit the surface of the sea before lifting clear and landing ashore. Ely was not put off by this narrow escape and decided to try landing on a ship. This time the cruiser *Pennsylvania* was chosen and a wooden platform 37m (120 ft) built over the rear deck. On 18th January 1911 Ely took off from a shore base and landed on the platform with 15m (50 ft) to spare. To help him stop in a short distance, ropes had been stretched across the platform in such a way that hooks, fitted near the aircraft's wheels, caught them. The *arrester* ropes were tied to heavy sandbags which slowed the aeroplane down. In order to assist take-offs, catapults were devised: the Wright brothers had used a simple one in 1904–5 but in 1912 a compressed-air powered catapult was introduced by the US Navy.

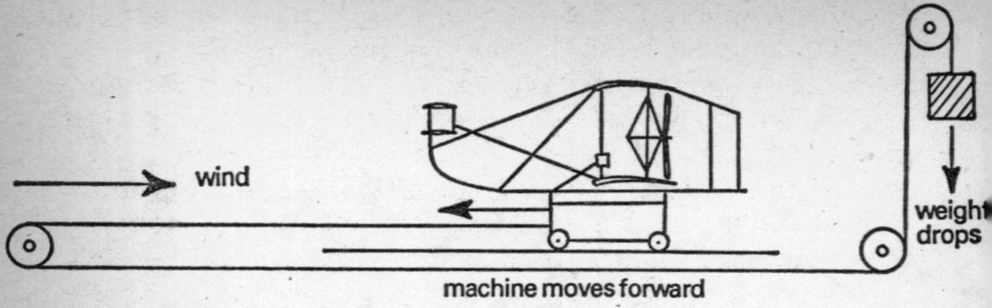

The Wright brothers' catapult, 1908. *Modern catapults use steam instead of a falling weight.*

During the First World War several ships were converted to carry seaplanes and landplanes but the first really successful aircraft carrier was HMS *Argus* completed in September 1918. The *Argus* had an unobstructed flight deck 168m (550 ft) long and carried the first squadron of aircraft which could drop aerial torpedoes. The war ended before *Argus* and her Sopwith Cuckoos were ready for action. Between the wars, naval aviation progressed

Naval aircraft

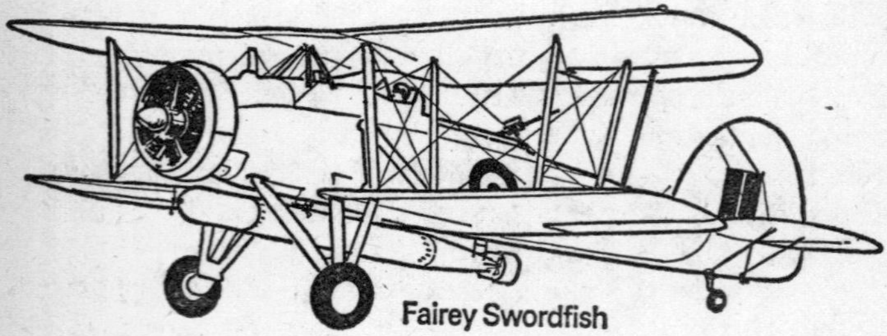

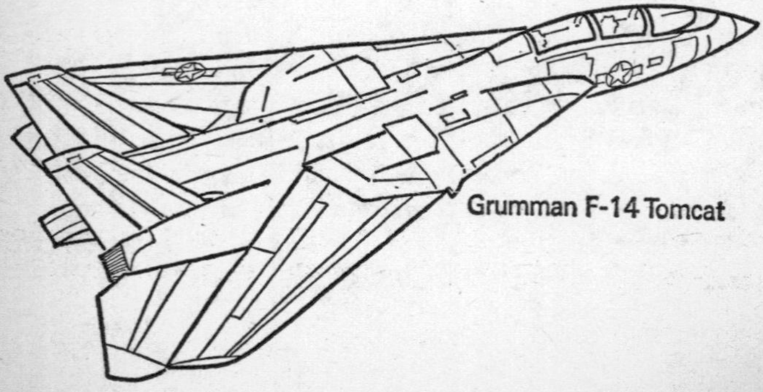

but rather slowly, for instance the Cuckoo was replaced by another slow biplane, the long-serving Fairey Swordfish. Aircraft were useful as 'spotters' but as most Admirals were convinced that the battleship was the most powerful ship afloat – despite the fact that US Army bombers had sunk an old unmanned German battleship in 1921 – they underestimated the usefulness of aircraft carriers.

During the Second World War the battleship faded out and aircraft carriers became the most important ships in any fleet. In December 1941 the Japanese attacked and almost destroyed the United States fleet at Pearl Harbor. The spearhead of the Japanese attack was six aircraft carriers carrying dive-bombers, fighter-bombers and torpedo-dropping aircraft. The Americans recovered and the great naval battles of the Pacific were fought between fleets of aircraft carriers. Since the war, fleets have been reduced in size but the aircraft carried on board the remaining carriers have become more powerful. For example the US Navy's Grumman F-14 Tomcat can attack six targets at the same time with its guided missiles.

Army Co-operation aircraft

Right from the early days of aviation, army experts saw that aircraft might prove to be useful new weapons and competitions were held to try out these flying machines. At the British Military Aeroplane Competition held on Salisbury Plain during 1912 as many as thirty-one aeroplanes entered: only ten finished the course. The winner was the colourful ex-cowboy Colonel S. F. Cody with his huge biplane called the *Cathedral*. During the First World War aeroplanes helped the army directly with three kinds of operation – reconnaissance missions, communications flights carrying passengers or messages, and attacks on enemy ground forces.

These operations were so successful that in the years between the wars, Army Co-operation squadrons were a permanent feature of the RAF. They worked very closely with the soldiers on the ground and carried out some very tricky feats – often in dangerous country such as the North-west Frontier of India. Important messages were picked up by a low-flying aircraft trailing a hook so that it caught a string stretched between two posts and tied to a

Army co-operation aircraft

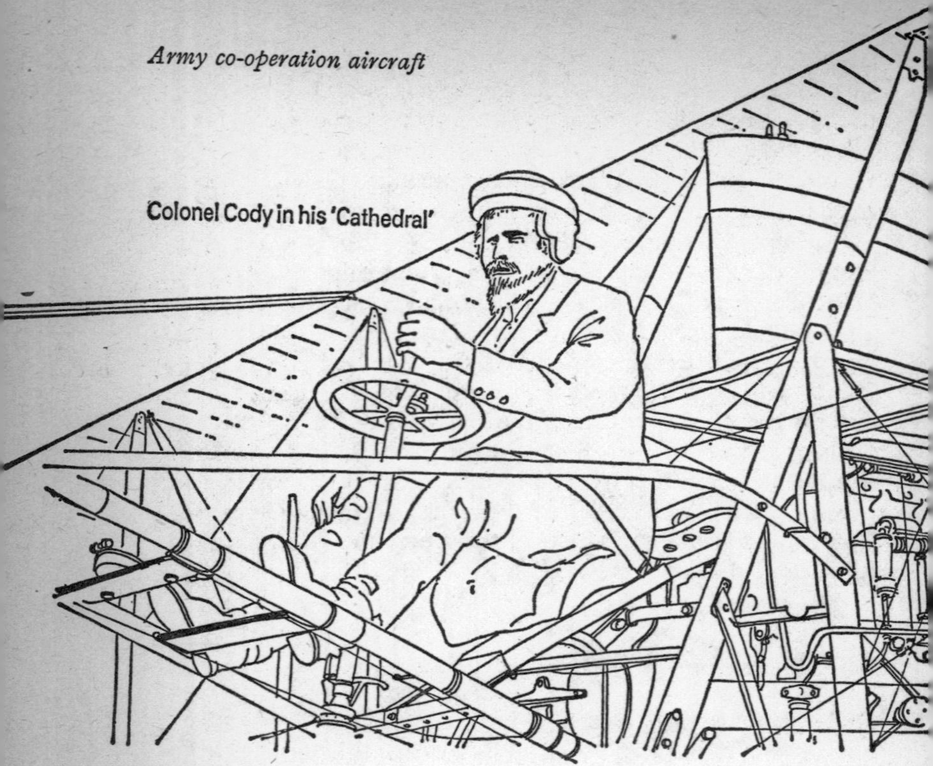

Colonel Cody in his 'Cathedral'

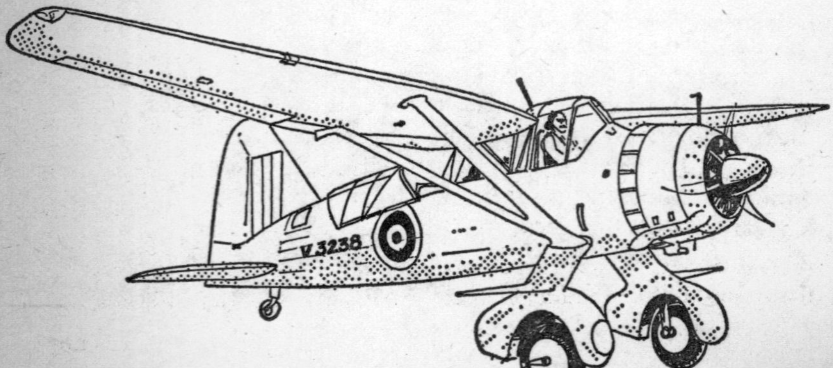

Westland Lysander

message bag. Supplies were flown to soldiers stationed in isolated outposts and this usually meant landing on a short, rough piece of ground or dropping the items by parachute. *General purpose* biplanes were often used for this work, such as the Hawker Audax developed from the Hart bomber, but in the 1930s a specially designed high-wing monoplane entered service with the RAF: this was the Westland Lysander. The Lysander was a real maid-of-all-work and served throughout the Second World War doing anything from towing targets to landing spies behind enemy lines.

In recent years Army Co-operation operations have continued with helicopters taking over many of the jobs previously tackled by slow-flying aeroplanes like the Lysander. Helicopters have the great advantage of being able to land in very small spaces or just hover in order to pick up a message or drop passengers. Helicopters are used in many roles, ranging from an ambulance to a gun-ship armed with machine guns or rockets. Aeroplanes still do some jobs for the army mainly in a *strike* role, attacking enemy forces with guns, bombs and rocket missiles.

The Royal Air Force

The story of the Royal Air Force begins with the Army. The Royal Engineers were responsible for observation balloons and kites during the early years of this century and in 1911 an Air Battalion of the Royal Engineers was formed. Then on 13th May 1912 this Air Battalion became part of the new service called the *Royal Flying Corps*, which consisted of four squadrons – three equipped with aeroplanes and one with airships and kites. A Naval *wing* was formed but in 1914 a separate *Royal Naval Air Service* was established. For most of the First World War the RFC and RNAS remained apart but on 1st April 1918 they were combined to form the *Royal Air Force.*

Between the Wars the RAF carried out the often dangerous duty of preserving law and order in some of the wilder territories of the British Empire. Other, pleasanter, operations included their very popular flying displays or 'Air Pageants' and competitions such as the Schneider Trophy seaplane races. All British military flying was under the control of the RAF, including the *Fleet Air*

Arm which operated from Navy warships. The Royal Navy were not happy with this arrangement and in 1937 the Fleet Air Arm was transferred to the Admiralty. Since this transfer the Royal Navy has retained control of naval aviation, which today involves many helicopters and some fixed-wing aircraft such as the Harrier vertical take-off fighter.

During the Second World War the RAF was divided into a number of *Commands*: Fighter, Bomber, and Coastal were the ones involved in active service but they were supported by several other Commands and Branches. In the late 1960s and the 1970s the RAF was completely reorganised and now consists of three Commands. Strike Command includes all the fighter, bomber, maritime reconnaissance and transport squadrons while Support Command concentrates on training, maintenance and research. The third Command operates the RAF's overseas squadrons in Germany.

The RAF celebrated its sixtieth anniversary in 1978 and many of the original squadrons remain, although their aircraft have changed dramatically. In 1918 No 1 Squadron were equipped with S.E.5A fighters and sixty years later they were flying Hawker Siddeley Harrier vertical take-off fighters. No 27 Squadron changed from the de Havilland D.H.4 day bomber to the delta-winged Avro Vulcan bomber powered by four jet engines. The R.E.8 biplanes of No 42 Squadron flew reconnaissance missions over France but their modern counterpart, the Hawker Siddeley Nimrod, patrols the oceans on maritime reconnaissance flights lasting twelve hours.

Training a pilot

Training a pilot to fly a modern jet fighter or bomber costs hundreds of thousands of pounds and, having learned, the pilot is in charge of an aircraft costing millions of pounds, so it is vitally important to choose the right man for the job. Prospective pilots have to undergo a series of tests and interviews lasting several days. These include a very thorough medical examination, searching interviews, aptitude tests and even an obstacle course. Only about one in five of the hopeful pilots is accepted for the first stage of training.

Hawk trainer

Learning to fly

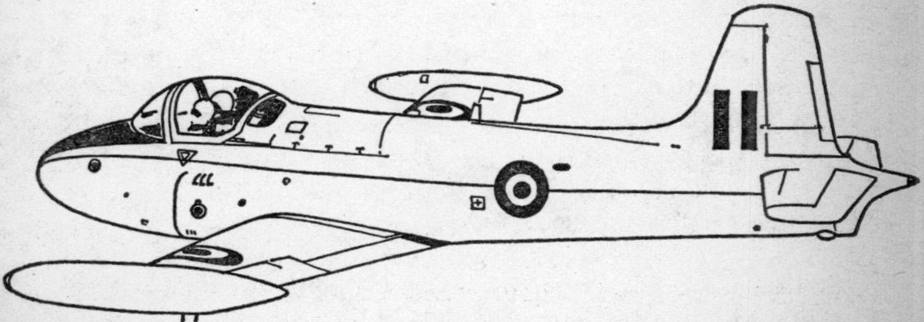

Jet Provost

Before a new recruit learns to fly, he (or she) is first taught to be an officer at an Officer Cadet Training Unit. This course involves sixteen weeks of very hard work both in the classroom and on the parade ground: a few more would-be pilots fail to make the grade. Those who graduate move on to a Flying Training School where at last they meet their first aircraft – a Scottish Aviation Bulldog. But for another six weeks or so the student is kept on the ground learning about aircraft and engines. Then the flying course begins.

On the first flight the student pilot has an easy time just getting the feel of the controls of the little Bulldog with his instructor sitting alongside. Then the programme gets steadily more difficult, starting with straight and level flying followed by gentle turns, take-offs and landings, building up to spinning and forced landings without an engine. After about fifteen hours the student makes his first solo flight, by which time he will probably have moved on to the next training aircraft, the BAC Jet Provost. As its name suggests the 'JP' is powered by a small jet engine, but it is capable of exceeding 660 km/h (400 mph) which is faster than a Spitfire. Even at this stage a student spends more time on the ground learning about flying than he spends in the air and he has some very difficult examinations to contend with. In the air he has to pass navigation and radio tests, complete low-level and night flying exercises, and he must be able to fly using only his instruments. When he reaches this very high standard the student is awarded his *Wings* – a great day in his life – but he has not nearly finished his training.

For the next stage the new pilot will probably fly a Hawker Siddeley Hawk, another jet trainer, which is considerably faster than the Jet Provost. Once he has become accustomed to this new machine he is taught to fly on practice operational missions including the use of weapons. Having completed this course the pilot moves on to an operational squadron where he learns to fly the front-line aircraft of the RAF.

Escape: parachutes and ejection seats

In the early days of aviation, up to and including the First World War, pilots did not carry parachutes so if their aircraft crashed

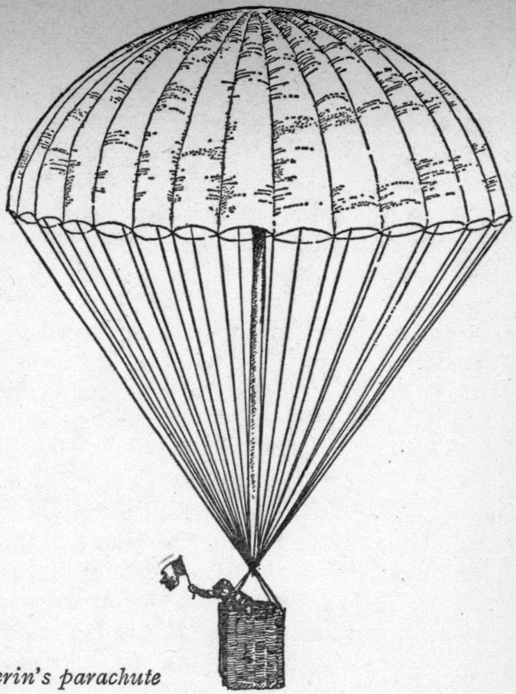

André Garnerin's parachute

they stayed with it. Of course these primitive aircraft flew relatively slowly so the chances of surviving a crash were much greater than with a modern high speed jet. The first descent by parachute was made from a balloon by a Frenchman, André Jacques Garnerin, as far back as 1797 but it was not until 1912 that anyone jumped from an aeroplane. The problem was to produce a parachute which could be folded into a small pack and yet open every time the *rip-cord* was pulled.

During the 1930s parachutes became a standard part of a service pilot's equipment and throughout the Second World War there was very little change. Fighter pilots usually wore their parachutes on their backs – low down so it formed a cushion for their seats. Other aircrew did not wear their parachutes all the time they were flying, instead they wore a harness and just clipped the parachute pack to the front of the harness should an emergency arise. To escape from a damaged aircraft the crew would open an escape hatch and 'bail out'. This worked well provided the aircraft was not travelling too quickly or flying near the ground. At high speeds the escaper did not have the strength to climb out against the force of the wind, and near the ground a parachute did not have time to open before the escaper hit the ground. A British invention overcame both these difficulties – the *ejection seat* developed by the Martin-Baker company. The complete seat was shot out of the aircraft by an explosive charge and the pilot then descended by parachute. The first trial of an ejection seat took place in 1946 when Bernard Lynch ejected from a Gloster Meteor flying at 515 km/h (320 mph).

Ejection seats were rapidly fitted to all high speed aircraft and many lives were saved. In 1955 two notable ejections were made successfully: an American test pilot escaped from a crashing Super Sabre which was flying at supersonic speed and an RAF officer made an experimental ejection from a Meteor which was taxiing along the ground. The ejection seat carried the officer high enough for his parachute to open before he reached the ground. Modern ejection seats are fully automatic after the pilot pulls a handle. The cockpit canopy is jettisoned, the seat shoots out, a small *drogue* parachute opens to steady the seat before the main parachute opens, the seat falls away and the pilot descends to safety.

Rockets and missiles

Rocket-powered missiles are by no means new, for the Chinese used rocket-propelled arrows in the thirteenth century. During the Napoleonic Wars, British forces bombarded Boulogne with some 2000 rockets designed by William Congreve. Congreve rockets were widely used in many parts of the world but they needed a stabilising stick (just like a giant firework rocket). William Hale eliminated this stick by making his rocket missiles spin, and this gave them stability. During the early years of the twentieth century a Russian called Konstantin Tsiolkovsky produced many new ideas for improved rockets including some powered by liquid fuels instead of gunpowder – but he never built one. The first successful liquid-fuelled rocket was built by the American rocket pioneer Robert H. Goddard in 1926. His rocket motor burned petrol in its own supply of oxygen, which was carried in liquid form: because rockets carry their own oxygen they can operate where there is no air – in outer space.

Escaping by ejection seat

During the 1930s German scientists and engineers led the way with rocket research and one of these was Dr Wernher von Braun who became one of the world's most famous rocket designers. He helped to design the V-2 rocket missile used during the Second World War by the Germans to attack targets in the south of England. It carried 1000 kg (1 ton) of high explosive and could reach targets 320 km (200 miles) away from its launching pad. Because it travelled at 5800 km/h (3600 mph) it could not be intercepted by fighter aircraft or shot down by guns. When the war ended most of the German rocket experts were encouraged to continue their work either in Russia or the United States. Von Braun went to the United States where he played a leading part in the American space programme including a major contribution to the Apollo-Saturn V liquid-fuelled rocket used for the moon landings.

In the years after the Second World War hundreds of rocket-propelled missiles were developed to carry out a host of different missions. There were huge rockets called ballistic missiles, such as the USA's Minuteman, which could carry a nuclear warhead from one continent to another. Smaller ballistic missiles were designed for land operations or to be carried aboard nuclear submarines, and these included the Polaris missile. These ballistic missiles were designed with their own navigation system which directed them on to their target, thus enabling them to hit moving targets such as aircraft or ships. Some were designed to seek out the heat from a jet engine while others carried their own radar or television to 'see' the target for themselves and 'home in' on it.

Modern missiles are incredibly complicated; for example, intercontinental ballistic missiles (ICBMs) can carry a number of nuclear warheads which can be released from the main missile out in space and directed against different targets. These are called MIRVs, or multiple, independently targetable re-entry vehicles. For each new type of missile a means of defeating it has to be invented, consequently anti-ballistic missile systems (ABM) were developed. Then a means of defeating the ABM system had to be devised so some ICBMs were fitted with decoy missiles ejected before the MIRVs. The missile race has become so expensive that most countries are trying to agree on a formula for limiting these fearful weapons.

1 *Rocket warfare 1944 – the German V-2*
2 *Rocket warfare 1960*

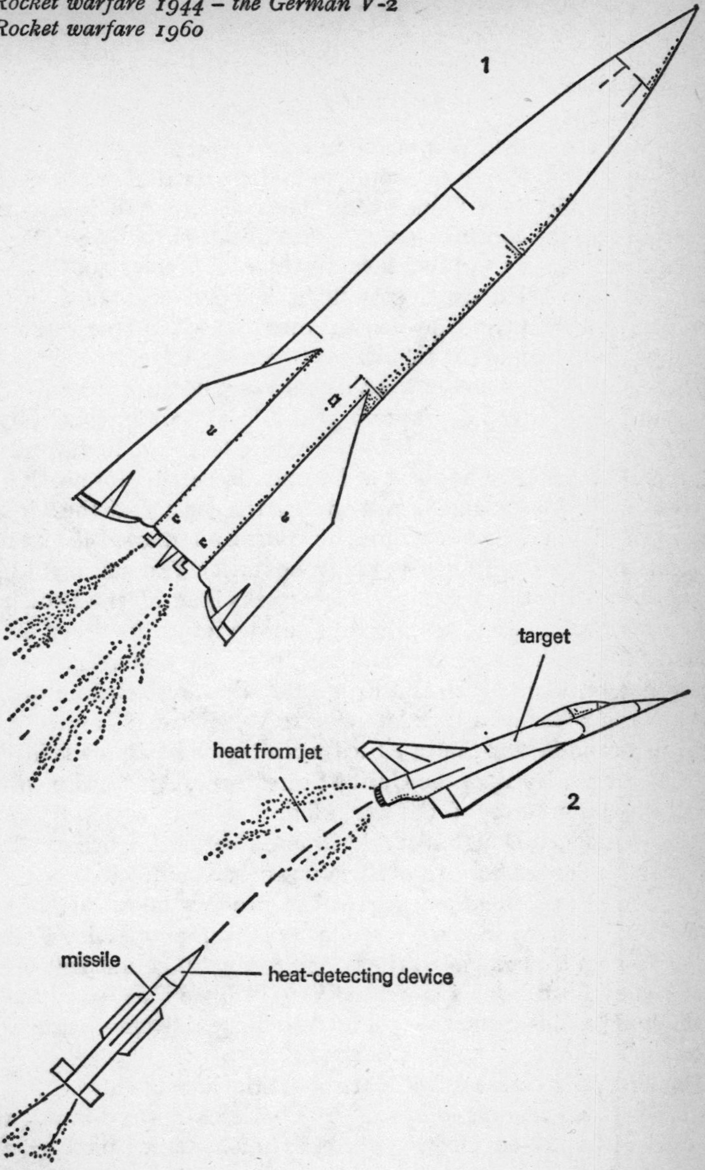

5 Work and Play

Record breakers

When the First World War ended in 1918 many pilots were demobilised from the services only to find it very difficult to settle into routine office jobs. Some of these airmen turned their attention to conquering the continents and oceans of the world by air. The lure of the Atlantic attracted several – especially as £10,000 had been offered for the first non-stop flight. The Atlantic was first crossed by air in May 1919 when an American flying-boat reached Portugal, but it landed at the Azores to refuel. A few days later, on 14th June 1919, a converted Vickers Vimy bomber took off from Newfoundland piloted by Captain John Alcock and navigated by Lieutenant Arthur Whitten Brown. Despite fog, rain, high winds and ice, they reached the coast of Ireland after flying for nearly sixteen hours. Alcock and Brown crossed the coast near the wireless station at Clifden only a few miles off course, a remarkable feat of navigation after covering 3043 km (1890 miles). The first flight in the opposite direction was made a few weeks later by the British airship R34 which then went on to make the return journey.

Many epic flights were made in these post-war years. The Australian brothers Keith and Ross Smith flew from Britain to Australia in 1919 and a year later Pierre Van Ryneveld and Quintin Brand flew to South Africa, both flights being made in Vickers Vimys. By 1924 the United States Army Air Service was ready to attempt a round-the-world flight, in short stages. Four specially designed Douglas 'World Cruisers' set out on 6th April and by 28th September two of the aircraft had completed the 42,398-km (26,345-mile) journey. Another round-the-world flight made headline news in 1931, when an American pilot Wiley Post and his navigator completed the trip in 8 days 16 hours. Two years later, Wiley Post flew his Lockheed Vega *Winnie Mae* round the world again and became the first man to make this long journey solo.

The long ocean crossings still attracted the intrepid airmen. The Pacific was conquered in 1928 by Charles Kingsford-Smith and his crew in a three-engined Fokker F.VII monoplane called

Record-breaking bombers
Vickers Vimy – first non-stop Atlantic flight, 1919.

Boeing B-52 jet bombers flew round the world non-stop in 45 hours in 1957. Here one is refuelling in flight.

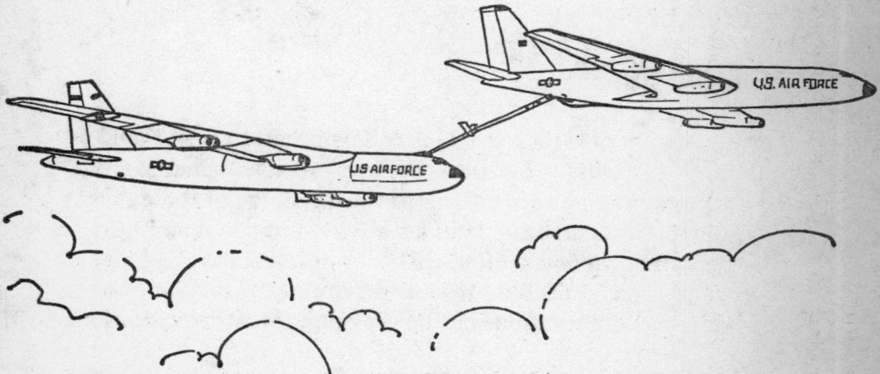

Southern Cross. In 1927 Charles Lindbergh flew solo from New York to Paris in 33½ hours and became an overnight hero. Women pilots joined the men and keen competition developed to set up the fastest time from place to place. One of the most famous women pilots was Amy Johnson who flew from England to Australia in 1930. At one stage Amy was beating the record held by the Australian pilot Bert Hinkler, then delays on the latter stages of the flight ruled out a record, but she did become the first woman to fly solo to Australia.

As the years go by, it becomes more difficult to find new records to establish; however, in 1949, a United States Boeing B-50 Superfortress made the first non-stop flight around the world – it was refuelled in flight four times. Eight years later three Boeing B-52 jet bombers flew in formation round the world without stopping and completed the trip in just over 45 hours. Long distance solo flights still attract a few enthusiastic pilots such as the British airwoman Sheila Scott, who flew solo around the world in 1966 setting a woman's record of just over 33 days. She also broke many other records with her long-distance solo flights. The veteran American pilot Max Conrad also broke many records and made a remarkable flight, flying solo round the world over both the North and South Poles. But transatlantic flights are frequently in the news and in 1974 a United States Lockheed SR-71A Blackbird flew from New York to London in the amazing time of 1 hour 55 minutes and 42 seconds.

Pioneering flights

Following the era of record breaking, pilots began to turn their attention towards flights of discovery, and previously inaccessible areas of the globe were surveyed from the air. Some of these flights were also notable as first flights but many were made mainly to survey the unknown areas, often with a view to establishing air routes across them. Suitable sites for aerodromes or seaplane bases were sought and observations on the prevailing weather conditions made.

Through the centuries many sailors searched Arctic waters for a short cut, known as the 'North-west Passage' to the Far East. The possibilities of flying from Europe to the Far East via the polar

Alan Cobham lands on the Thames after flying to Australia and back in 1926

regions were considered many years before passenger flights started. There were two unsuccessful attempts to reach the North Pole by air: the first by balloon in 1897 and the second by flying boat in 1925. Then in 1926 two expeditions were preparing for an attempt at the same time. There was great rivalry between the American team, led by Admiral Richard Byrd and Floyd Bennett using a three-engined Fokker F.VII equipped with skis, and the Norwegian Roald Amundsen with an airship flown by its Italian designer, General Umberto Nobile. Byrd flew from Spitzbergen to the North

The first flight over Mount Everest took place in 1933.

Pole and back on 9th May. Amundsen was one of the first to congratulate Byrd and, although disappointed, his party set out a day later in the airship. They reached the Pole and continued to Alaska and so made the first flight across the polar regions.

Many flights were made in the northern polar regions during the following years to investigate the possibilities of using this route for airliners. In 1933 an American airline sent the famous pilot Charles Lindbergh to survey this route but he returned with a very pessimistic report. In the barren lands of the north there were not sufficient aerodrome sites for the short-range airliners available at that time. It was not until 1954 that passengers were first carried on a regular service across the polar regions when the Scandinavian airline S.A.S. linked Copenhagen with Los Angeles.

Flying in the Antarctic did not arouse as much interest as the Arctic because it was not on a possible air route, but it was an unknown region which could most easily be explored from the air. Sir Hubert Wilkins led expeditions in 1928 and 1929 which used two aircraft equipped with skis to survey Graham Land. Admiral Richard Byrd then arrived on the scene with a very well equipped expedition which included four aircraft. After several survey flights, Byrd flew over the South Pole on 28th November 1929.

One of the greatest pioneers of the airways was Sir Alan Cobham who set out to prove that the aeroplane could fly thousands of miles and keep to a time schedule. He also surveyed the most suitable routes and possible airfields along them. Between 1924 and 1928 Cobham made out-and-return flights to Rangoon, Cape Town and Sydney and also made a 32,200-km (20,000-mile) flight round Africa. These flights had to be carefully planned: there were few aerodromes available, consequently petrol and other supplies had to be transported to the proposed landing sites. Owing to this shortage of aerodromes, Cobham used a floatplane and flying boat for the two longest flights because he could usually find a suitable stretch of water on which to land.

During 1933 a pioneering flight of a very different nature was made, for in that year two specially prepared aeroplanes flew over the summit of Mount Everest, which is 8848 m (29,028 feet) high. The object of the flight was to photograph the formidable mountain which was not conquered from the ground until 1953. Aerial photography was not new but pilots had rarely encountered such intense cold and high winds.

Air racing

The airmen who made daring flights across oceans were pitting their skills and their machines against the forces of nature. Other pilots preferred to challenge each other and take part in conventional races. During the years before the First World War great flying displays were held and these often included races in which the competing aircraft had to fly around a course marked on the ground with pylons. Longer races were also held and often the prizes were offered by newspapers because aviation had become a popular sport. The American publisher James Gordon Bennett sponsored races for balloons and aeroplanes, while in Britain the *Daily Mail* offered several large prizes including £10,000 to the winner of the Circuit of Britain race in 1911. This was won by a French pilot, Lieutenant de Vaisseau Conneau, flying a French Blériot monoplane: in fact only two aircraft completed the course

The first Schneider Trophy winner of 1913, the Deperdussin.

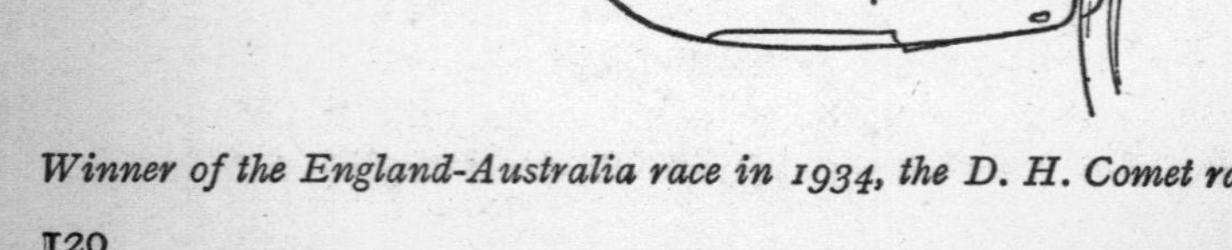

Winner of the England-Australia race in 1934, the D. H. Comet racer.

within the time limit and both were French. The *Daily Mail* Aerial Derby of 1912 involved flying round London and again a French Blériot won, but this time flown by a British pilot, T. O. M. Sopwith, who became a leading manufacturer of aeroplanes.

A special race for seaplanes was organised in 1913 and a prize was presented by a wealthy Frenchman called Jacques Schneider. The seaplanes were not going to race against each other, but against the clock, in other words each one was timed as it flew the agreed number of laps around the course. The first winner was a little French Deperdussin monoplane with a speed of 73.63 km/h (45.75 mph), and the second Schneider Trophy race, held in 1914, was won by a British Sopwith Tabloid. After the First World War the Schneider Trophy continued until 1931 when it was won for the third time in a row by Britain which therefore won it outright. The last winning seaplane was a Supermarine S.6B, forerunner of the Spitfire, with a speed of 547.31 km/h (340.08 mph).

In the 1920s circuit racing and long distance races attracted large entries and made headline news. Circuit racing was very popular in the United States where there were several major trophies to be won. In Britain there was even an Oxford versus Cambridge University air race held in 1921 – which Cambridge won easily. A major British air race started in 1922 when King George V presented a cup to encourage British designers and pilots. The first King's Cup Air Race was flown from Croydon to Glasgow and back, and was won by Captain F. L. Barnard at 198.9 km/h (123.6 mph). The King's Cup continued and many famous pilots won this coveted trophy – which is still a fixture in the air-racing calendar.

One of the most spectacular long-distance races of all time was the MacRobertson Race between England and Australia held in 1934. After an exciting race the winner was a de Havilland Comet racer flown by C. W. A. Scott and T. Campbell-Black, which reached Melbourne in only 2 days 23 hours. This Comet was one of three specially designed for the race, but the machines which came second and third in the race were a Douglas DC-2 and a Boeing 247 – both American airliners. Another similar race was held in 1953, this time to New Zealand, and the winner was an English Electric Canberra jet bomber which reached Christchurch in just under 24 hours.

Air racing on a grand scale has become very expensive and

amateur pilots have organised their sport to try and keep costs down. In the United States racing aeroplanes designed to a formula, like racing cars, have been introduced. For instance, Formula V aircraft must be fitted with Volkswagen car engines. In Britain, where there are relatively few racing aeroplanes, most events are run as handicaps with the slower aeroplanes starting first: if the handicapper has done his sums correctly then they should all cross the finishing line together!

Records

The records created by the early pilots were simply ones of duration – a few minutes or even seconds spent in the air. Then came speed, height and distance records, and these were followed by a complicated set of records for different kinds of aeroplane carrying a variety of loads. But of all these records the one which has captured the imagination of the public over the years has been the world air speed record. The first holder was Alberto Santos-Dumont, a popular Brazilian who designed and flew his own airships and aeroplanes in France. In 1906 Santos-Dumont achieved a speed of 41.27 km/h (25.64 mph) with his tail-first aeroplane called '14 bis'. It became obvious that rules had to be made to control record attempts and in 1905 the Fédération Aéronautique Internationale (FAI) was founded by eight nations with its headquarters in Paris. Their rules for the world speed record stated that four runs (two in each direction) had to be made over a 3-kilometre (1.86-mile) course and the average speed worked out. During these runs, the aeroplane had to remain below 75 m (250 ft) to help the timekeepers – who had to be officially approved. The first speed record ratified by the FAI was Paul Tissandier's speed of 54.77 km/h (34.03 mph) flying a Wright biplane. Apart from the American Glenn Curtiss, who held the record for a short time in 1909, all the world speed

Opposite page
1 Santos-Dumont (1906); 41.27 km/h (25.64 mph).
2 Messerschmitt Bf. 109R (1939); 755.14 km/h (469.14 mph)
3 Gloster Meteor (1945); 975.68 km/h (606.26 mph).
4 North American X-15 (1967); 7,279 km/h (4,534) mph.

1

2

3

4

record holders from 1907 to 1914 were French, and by 1914 the record stood at 203.81 km/h (126.64 mph). Between the World Wars the record increased from 275.22 km/h (171.01 mph) to 754.97 km/h (469.17 mph) and at various times it was held by France, USA, Britain, Italy and Germany. After the Second World War, jet aircraft began breaking records, starting with the Gloster Meteor in 1945. Speeds rose steadily until they passed the 1,000 km/h (620 mph) mark, but at this point a double problem emerged. Pilots found it dangerous to fly at this speed below 75 metres and timekeepers had trouble timing a 3-kilometre run which took only ten seconds to complete. A new rule was introduced in 1951 allowing a 15- to 25-kilometre course, with just two runs and at any altitude. The record shot up and by 1976 it stood at 3523.00 km/h (2189.00 mph) held by an American Lockheed SR-71A – but even this has been beaten by American rocket-powered aircraft on research flights which did not comply with FAI regulations.

The first world altitude record for aeroplanes was established in 1909 with a flight at 155m (508 ft) – which is lower than the Post Office Tower in London. The pilot was an Englishman, Hubert Latham, flying a French Antoinette aeroplane in France. Latham later held the record several times, ending with 1384m (4540 ft). Of course, balloons had been higher than any of these aeroplane flights: even before the Wright brothers' first flight in 1903 a hydrogen balloon had reached a height of 10,800 m (35,433 ft). The FAI introduced special classes for balloons, airships, aeroplanes, rotary-winged aircraft (e.g. helicopters) and gliders. Balloons and aeroplanes have vied with each other for the absolute height record over the years with the balloon leading the way until the introduction of the modern high-flying jet and rocket-powered aeroplanes. In 1973 a Russian Mikoyan E-266 took off and climbed to a height of 36,240 m (118,898 ft) which established a world record. American rocket-powered aircraft have exceeded this height but they cannot claim an official record because they were launched from other aircraft.

The world record for distance in a straight line has involved many epic flights, some of which have already been mentioned, such as Charles Lindbergh's solo flight from New York to Paris in 1927 – a distance of 5809 km (3609 miles). Refuelling in flight is not allowed but, even so, modern jets have an extremely long range;

for instance, in 1962 a Boeing B-52 bomber flew from Okinawa in the Pacific to Madrid in Spain, a distance of 20,169 km (12,532 miles). Such flights have become a test of organisation and equipment rather than a test of the physical endurance of the pioneers.

Aerobatics

In the early days of aviation some pilots threw their flimsy aeroplanes about the sky to amuse the crowds at air displays and this was known as 'stunting' or 'aerial acrobatics'. Today the name has changed to *aerobatics* but crowds at air displays still watch enthralled as aeroplanes perform manoeuvres undreamed of by the pioneers. In addition, aerobatics has become a competitive sport with pilots from many nations competing against each other in specially designed aeroplanes.

Aerobatics

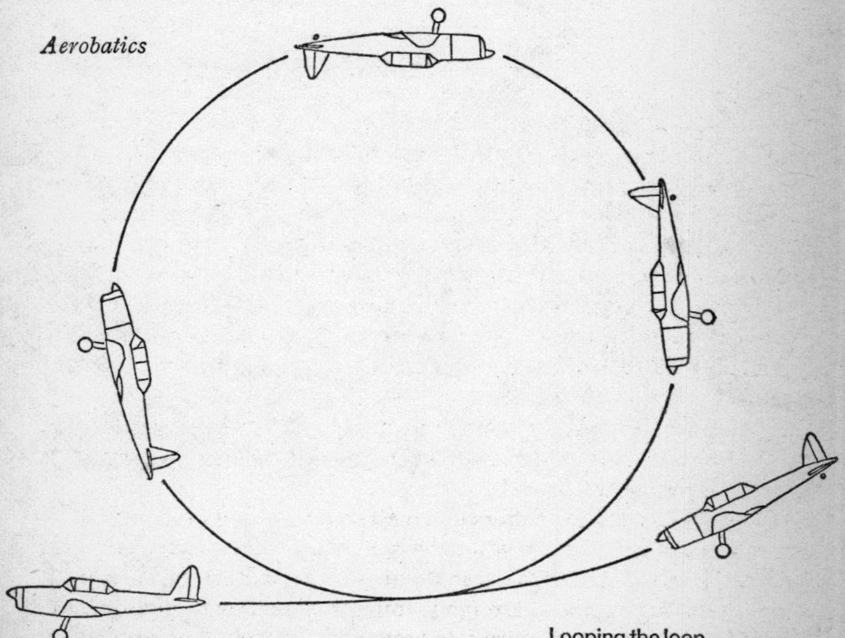

Looping the loop

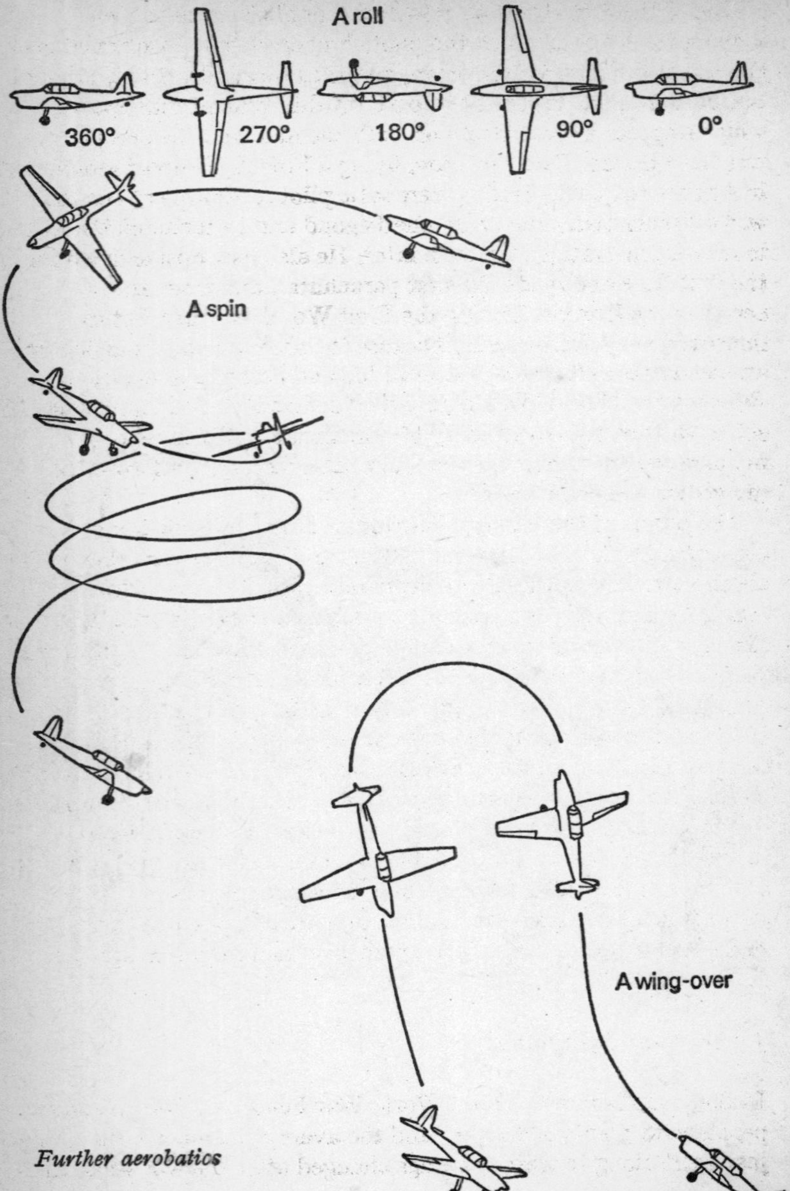

Further aerobatics

One of the first stunts to attract the public's attention was looping the loop, in which the pilot climbed steeply, continued over the top of the loop upside down, and then descended to his original line of flight. The first pilot to perform this difficult manoeuvre, which imposes a great strain on both the man and the aeroplane, was the Russian, Petr Nesterov, flying a French Nieuport monoplane in August 1913. The leading aerobatic pilot in Europe at the time was a Frenchman called Adolphe Pégoud and he included the loop in his demonstrations a month later. He also flew upside down for the first time and made the first parachute jump from an aeroplane in Europe. During the First World War aerobatics improved very dramatically because the ability to out-manoeuvre an enemy aircraft was a matter of life and death in a 'dog-fight'. Between the World Wars aerobatic displays included loops, rolls, spins, wing-overs, inverted flight and variations of these basic manoeuvres. Also popular were aerobatic displays by formations of fighters – usually biplanes.

The power of the jet engine introduced new possibilities in aerobatic displays because jet fighters and trainers were able to climb vertically upwards with apparent ease. Military display teams regularly give spectacular aerobatic demonstrations at air displays and one of the most successful over the years has been the RAF's 'Red Arrows'. Their red Gnat jet trainers flying in formation or in pairs have earned a high reputation for precision flying. But the jets are not alone in aerobatic team flying, for the Rothmans company have sponsored a small team of propeller-driven biplanes. These Pitts Specials are capable of some incredible manoeuvres, for instance the aeroplane falls head over heels and then suddenly recovers. Aerobatic pilots capable of flying in one of these teams or able to compete in the World Championships must be not only gifted pilots but also perfectionists prepared to practise their manoeuvres time after time as there is no margin for error.

Joy rides and flying clubs

In the years before the First World War flying as a hobby was for people with plenty of money, and the average member of the public just went along to watch. Things changed after the war when there

1

2

1 Joyriding with Alan Cobham's Circus
2 Club flying in 1927
3 Flying Flea
4 Cessna 150

3

4

was a determined effort to get more people into the air: joy rides, flying clubs and home-built aeroplanes were all available at modest prices.

A leading figure in these days was Alan Cobham (later to become Sir Alan Cobham) who toured the country with his 'flying circus'. In addition to aerobatic displays, his pilots took people up for a 'Ten-bob flip' (i.e. 10 shillings = 50p). These trips were extremely popular and for thousands of people this experience sparked off a lifelong interest in aviation. In 1925 the Government decided to help flying clubs in Britain and in this way encourage more people to train as pilots. Flying clubs were founded near most large towns and many light aircraft were built for amateur pilots: these could be bought for little more than the price of a motor car. One of the most popular light aircraft of this period was the de Havilland Moth biplane which was followed by the Gipsy Moth and the Tiger Moth. Amy Johnson used a Gipsy Moth for her famous solo flight to Australia in 1930. A flying club had made the whole thing possible for Amy was not well-off: she joined the London Aeroplane Club where she learned to fly in her spare time, and then she qualified as a mechanic with the Club. The popularity of flying clubs continued to increase in the 1930s and the number of clubs in Britain increased from just over 400 in 1928 to well over 1500 by 1933.

The idea of an aeroplane which could be built in the garage of the average handyman was very strong in the 1930s. A French designer, Henri Mignet, designed a small and simple aeroplane called a Pou du Ciel or Flying Flea. The Flea was easy to construct and many were being built in the mid-1930s when a serious defect was discovered: it was difficult to pull out of a steep dive. The dream of many hopeful pilots came to an end.

The Second World War brought private flying to a halt. When peace returned in 1945 some of the clubs re-emerged but the cost of flying in Britain has never returned to the levels of the 1930s. In the United States the story is very different, for private aircraft are extremely popular and flying is relatively inexpensive. The term *General Aviation* (G.A.) is used to cover private, business, air-taxi and all other branches of aviation other than military and airline operations. There are some 200,000 G.A. aircraft in the world today and of these 75 per cent operate in the USA. The modern equivalent of the de Havilland Moth is the American Cessna 150 which first flew in 1957, and in only ten years the number built had passed the 10,000 mark. The 150 is a high-wing monoplane with a 100 horsepower engine and it can carry two people in comfort at a cruising speed of 188 km/h (117 mph).

Flying doctors and aerial ambulances

When someone is seriously ill they need attention quickly, and this usually means getting a doctor to the patient or transferring the patient to hospital. In a village, town or city this is not a problem but in a very remote area fast travel becomes a matter of life or death. In some parts of Australia, Africa and South America there are settlements where the only method of reaching civilisation used to be by a long ride on horseback. Aviation has provided the answer to their problem and they now have a flying doctor service.

Australia has one of the best schemes, called the Royal Flying Doctor Service, which was founded in 1926. The problem was twofold – poor surface transport and no telephone system. To improve communications, isolated farms were equipped with radio transmitter-receivers, but many of them did not have any electricity either so they had to make their own by driving a generator fitted with bicycle pedals. Once the farmers could radio for help, aircraft were hired from the local airlines to fly out a doctor or transport the patient to hospital. Aerial ambulances are also used in Britain to rescue patients in the Highlands and Islands of Scotland. A normal airline service can easily be diverted to pick up a patient in an emergency, or a special helicopter flight might be ordered if the patient is stranded on a mountain or at sea.

In the United States a new rescue service has been introduced in recent years using para-rescuemen. These highly trained men drop by parachute to help anyone in trouble, but one of their most important tasks has been to recover space capsules and astronauts after their journeys into space. The para-rescuemen have to be trained in many skills including parachuting, first aid, mountaineering, Arctic survival and skin-diving.

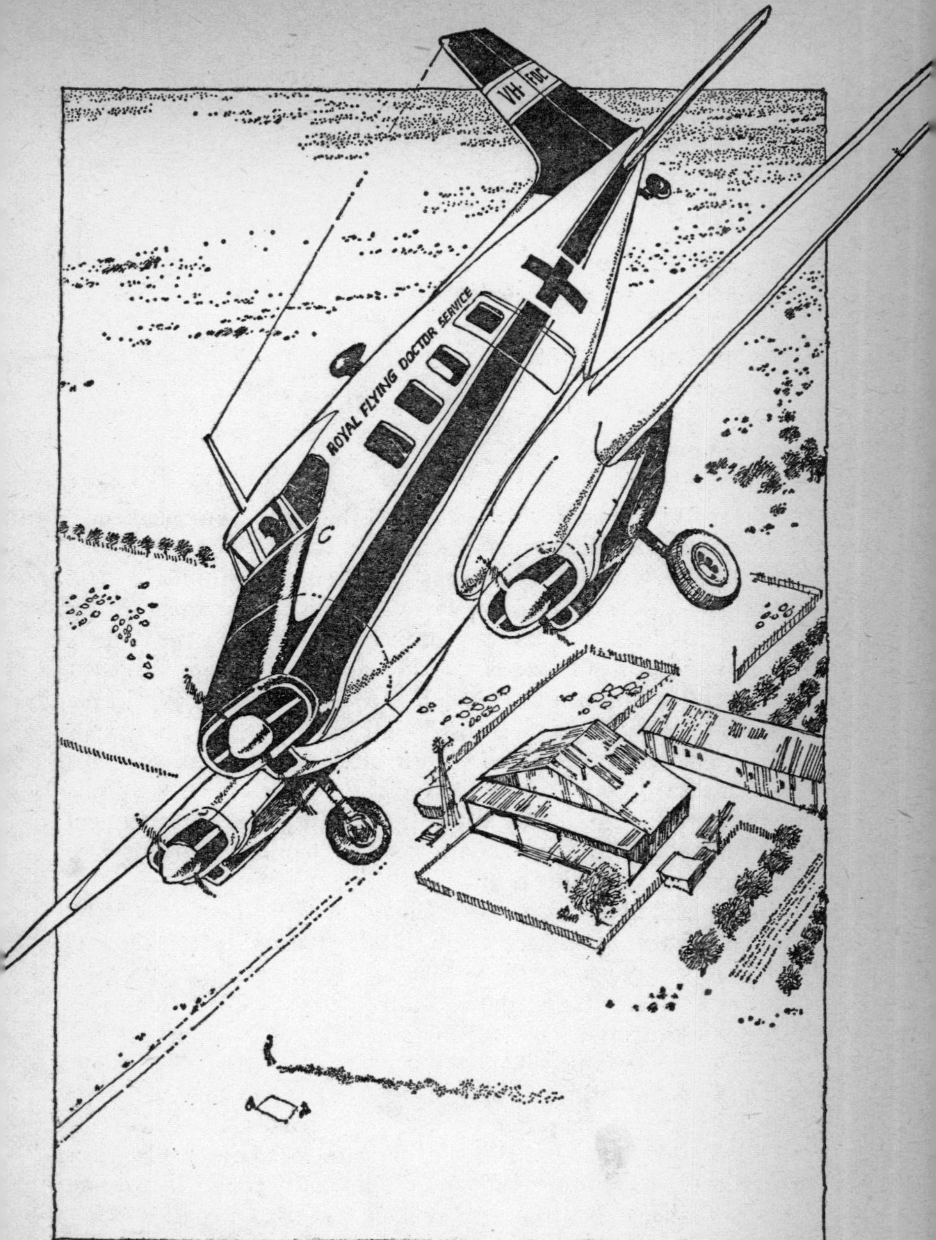
ROYAL FLYING DOCTOR SERVICE
VH-FDC

Business aircraft

In the world of business it is often said that 'time is money' and this includes travelling time which, as far as the company is concerned, is wasted time. For instance, travelling from one factory to another 400 km (250 miles) away by train or car can absorb one day in each direction – so three days are needed for a one-day visit. By air it is possible to travel this distance in an hour or so, do a day's work and return the same day. After the Second World War business aircraft began to be used more and more, especially as smaller companies combined to form large corporations capable of financing an aircraft or fleet of aircraft. In some cases the aircraft was bought for the top executive's use but it proved so successful that further aircraft were acquired so that more key personnel could save on travelling time.

In the United States, where distances are even more of a problem than in Britain, business aircraft are widely used. Many executives have jet aircraft converted for their use, each complete with desk, telephone, typewriter, conference table and even a bar. Some extremely wealthy executives and oil millionaires own jet airliners converted for their personal use with luxurious fittings including a bed and even a bathroom. Most executive aircraft, however, are more modest, carrying from four to twelve passengers. In Britain de Havilland's Dove and Heron of the late 1940s were widely used as executive aircraft and they were followed by the small twin-jet Hawker Siddeley HS.125 (de Havilland had become part of the Hawker Siddely group by this time). The HS.125 can cruise at 800 kph (500 mph) and it has even sold in America – the home of the business aircraft! The choice of aircraft in America is very wide, and competition for sales is very fierce. For instance one company, Cessna, offer about forty different models, ranging from the two-seater Model 150 to their Model 500 Citation powered by two jet engines.

Flying farmers and cowboys

Back in the 1920s farmers in the United States took to the air to wage war on insects which were eating their crops. Old biplanes flew low over the fields, dropping a stream of powder which fell on the crops and killed the insects. *Dusting* crops from an aircraft had two advantages over the more conventional tractor: it was faster and it did not damage the crops with its wheels. On the other hand, aircraft were more expensive than tractors. It was not until the 1950s, when many old warplanes were available at low prices, that the aeroplane became widely used as a farm implement. These old aeroplanes were converted to carry chemicals, either in powder form for dusting or as a liquid for spraying. The actual chemical varied according to the job to be tackled but usually it was some type of pest-destroyer or fertiliser. The dropping of fertiliser or *top dressing* was developed in New Zealand where barren hills were converted to grass pastures for grazing sheep by dropping the much needed phosphate fertiliser from the air. In the United States farmers pioneered the dropping of seeds from the air and large areas were sown with wheat and rice: in fact almost all the North American rice crop is now seeded from the air.

The early agricultural aircraft were all secondhand machines converted for their new work. This involved fitting a large tank or *hopper* into the fuselage and mounting the spraying or dusting gear along the wings. The aircraft converted in this way ranged from small de Havilland Tiger Moths to Boeing B-17 Flying Fortress bombers. Helicopters were also used and they had two advantages: they could operate in confined spaces such as narrow valleys, and the *downwash* from their rotor blades helped to blow the chemical right into the heart of the crop. During the 1960s farming by air became a very successful business and aircraft were specially produced for this difficult work. The resulting aeroplanes were not

An agricultural aircraft spraying crops

very elegant because they had to carry all the external spraying gear and be strong enough to stand up to frequent landings on rough ground in order to recharge the hopper. The cockpits were carefully designed to keep out the chemicals and withstand a crash – accidents do happen, especially when the spraying *runs* are made just a few feet above the ground. Many of the successful agricultural aircraft have been built in the United States where they are widely used. The Fletcher FU-24 was one of the first to sell in large numbers, but there were also a number of rivals such as the Piper Pawnee, the Cessna Agwagon and the Grumman Ag-Cat biplane.

On some large farms and ranches aircraft have even replaced the car and horse. The modern cowboy has taken to the helicopter, which is very effective at rounding up stray cattle: though less romantic than the old image of a guitar-playing cowboy riding the range on his faithful steed. But aviation has changed many things – even the weather. In areas suffering from a drought, clouds have been *seeded* with a chemical and this has brought on the much-needed rain.

Surveying from the air

The Romans surveyed routes for their roads from convenient hilltops but modern surveyors are able to use aircraft, which provide an even better view and are mobile. From an aircraft we obtain a 'bird's eye view' of the earth and if this is photographed we have the beginnings of a map. Balloons and aeroplanes were used in this way for military purposes since their early days, but in the 1920s aerial map-making of the earth's surface got under way. With a camera pointing downwards, photographs were taken at regular intervals along a straight line. By timing the camera carefully the photographs were taken so that they overlapped slightly. Having completed one run, the aircraft returned alongside the original line and by flying to and fro in this way the required area was covered by a chequered pattern.

Modern map-makers still operate in the same way but their equipment has improved tremendously. This includes not only the camera but also the aircraft and the special machines for converting a photograph into a map. By taking stereoscopic photographs and

1

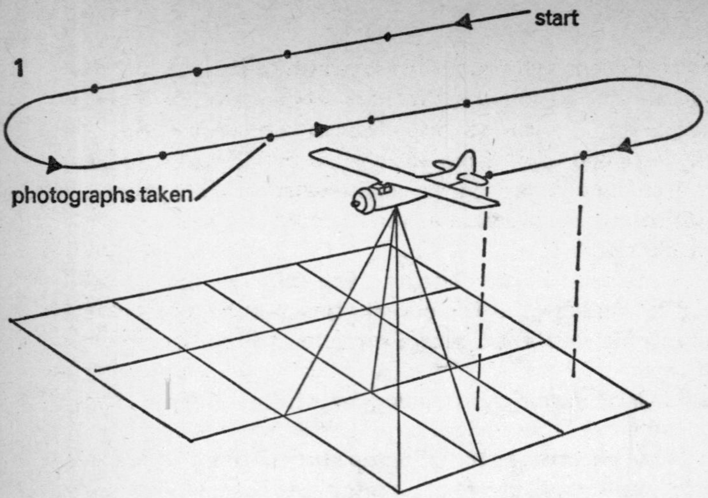

2

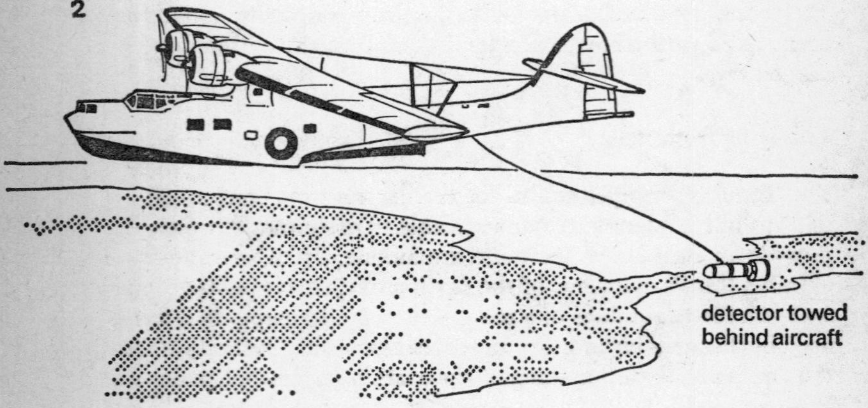

1 Aerial map-making
2 Canso amphibian searching for valuable ores

viewing these through a stereoscopic viewer the map-makers obtain a three-dimensional effect. This enables them to study hills and valleys which are represented on a map by *contour lines*. All this equipment is very expensive, but map-making from the air is so much quicker than the old methods with theodolites and measuring chains, especially if the area to be surveyed is marshy, mountainous or covered with trees.

Maps usually show what is visible on the surface of the earth, but geologists are interested in the materials beneath the surface. Aircraft are fitted out as flying laboratories carrying delicate instruments which record their information continuously during a survey flight. From these records the geologists can find out if there are any valuable minerals such as oil, uranium or iron ore beneath the earth's crust.

Even historians have taken to the air to study archaeological remains from one of the most modern forms of transport. Patterns of buildings, long since demolished, can often be seen from the air. Fields of oats reveal old buildings particularly well. Because the soil in the region of the building is often poorer than the surrounding area, the oats grow less well and so reveal the shape of the building. The Royal Air Force photographed Hadrian's Wall as a training exercise and archaeologists discovered several new camps. A detailed plan of one of the almost vanished settlements was produced which would have rivalled the one produced by the Roman surveyors centuries earlier.

Fighting fires

Because aircraft provide such excellent mobile viewpoints they are ideal for spotting forest fires. Trees are a valuable crop, grown to produce timber and wood pulp for paper-making, which a forest fire can destroy all too quickly. A fire which gets out of hand can also endanger human and animal life, so the effects of a forgotten camp fire or a lightning strike can be devastating.

In 1919 the United States Army Air Corps began to patrol forests in California and from this small beginning worldwide fire-spotting operations have grown. Pilots soon learned to spot fires almost before they happened by keeping an eye on campers and following in the path of any dangerous-looking thunderstorm. In the 1930s fire-fighting equipment was first dropped from the air to firemen on the ground. Then in the 1940s firemen were dropped by parachute in the region of the fire. This was rather dangerous, but the 'smoke-jumpers' got to the fire very quickly and, with luck, they could bring it under control before it had time to spread and become really dangerous. Since the Second World War

Water-bombing: a Canadair CL-215

helicopters have been introduced to carry firemen and their equipment to forest fires – or any other fire in a remote area.

A new method of fighting forest fires has been widely used in recent years and this is called *water-bombing*. Each aircraft is fitted with a large water tank and a release valve so the pilot can drop the water on a fire. One load is not usually sufficient so the pilot has to fill up his tank and return to the fire. Seaplanes are frequently used because there are usually lakes to be found in forest country – but no airfields. With a seaplane the pilot can

'*Smoke jumpers*'

alight on the lake and fill his tanks by scooping water up as the aircraft taxies into position for a quick take-off. The Canadian company Canadair designed an aircraft specifically for water-bombing. Their CL-215 is a twin-engined amphibious flying-boat which has very large tanks mounted in its fuselage capable of carrying 5455 litres (1200 gallons) of water – which is ten times as much as the earlier water-bombers. What is even more remarkable is the fact that these tanks can be filled, as the CL-215 skims across a lake, or the sea, in under 20 seconds.

Fun in the air

For many people the sea provides a place where they can enjoy themselves in one way or another, but for a smaller number of people the air is the place to indulge in a hobby or sport. The more usual aerial sporting activities such as ballooning, gliding, air racing and club flying have already been mentioned, but there are other ways of using the air.

The history of hang-gliders goes back to the 1890s but in recent years a new sport has emerged. The modern era of hang-gliding resulted from an invention which was part of the United States space programme. A folding wing was needed to carry spacecraft down to earth after they had re-entered the atmosphere. Francis Rogallo invented an A-shaped wing covered with strong fabric and this was adapted to produce a low cost portable hang-glider. The pilot was suspended in a harness beneath the wing and he held on to a bar rigidly attached to the wing. To control the glider he just moved his own weight about by bending or straightening his arms. Hang-gliding grew in popularity very rapidly because it was so cheap and gave people who had never flown before a chance to 'fly like a bird'. Some of these came to grief, but now that clubs have organised training programmes and laid down rules, there are fewer accidents. Although the Rogallo-type hang-glider is still popular, other shapes have been developed.

Parachutes were originally used to save lives but someone discovered that descending from an aeroplane could be an enjoyable experience, and parachuting as a sport was born. People who jump for pleasure always wear two parachutes just in case one fails to open. Beginners usually start by using a *static line* linking one of their parachutes to the aircraft: when they jump out the parachute opens automatically. (This method was used by paratroops during the Second World War.) As the parachutist grows more experienced, free falls can be attempted, in which the jumper delays opening his *canopy* for some time and enjoys falling through the air and performing simple acrobatics. Teams of free fall parachutists, with smoke canisters attached to their legs to make them visible, are a popular attraction at air displays. Contests for parachutists are judged by their style during the descent and the accuracy of their landing. The parachute canopies used in

Two hang gliders

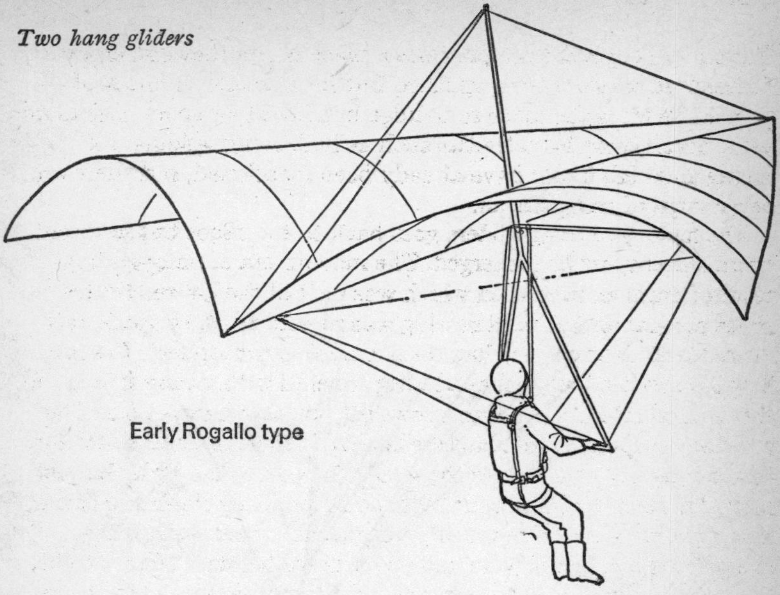

Early Rogallo type

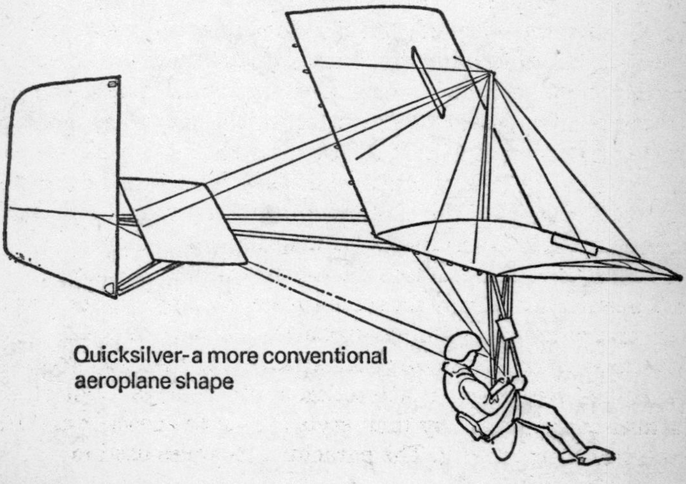

Quicksilver-a more conventional aeroplane shape

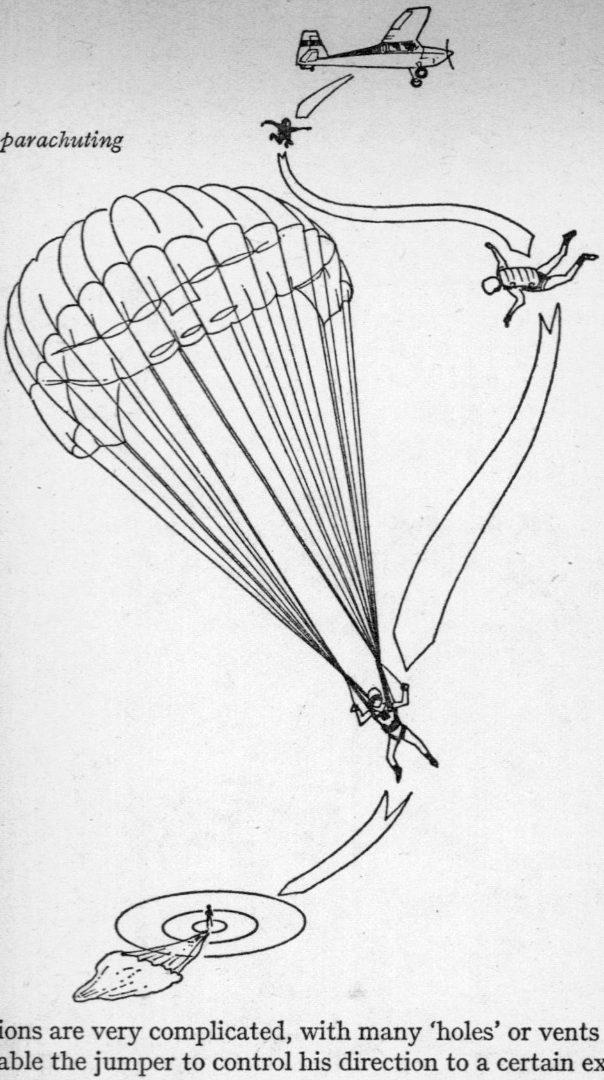

competitions are very complicated, with many 'holes' or vents which enable the jumper to control his direction to a certain extent.

A new variation of the parachute has emerged in recent years which, instead of descending, takes the 'jumper' up into the air. The participant starts on the ground with an open canopy and is then towed into the air – rather like a kite. The towing can be done by a car or a speedboat which makes *parascending* much less expensive than jumping from an aeroplane.

The future

Trying to forecast the future of aviation and space travel is a very difficult task and in the past many famous men have been proved hopelessly wrong with their predictions. In fact, the carefully considered opinions of engineers and scientists have usually been further from the truth than the fiction of writers such as Jules Verne and H. G. Wells. In 1896 the great physicist Lord Kelvin said '. . . I have not the smallest molecule of faith in aerial navigation other than ballooning. . . .' Seven years later the Wright brothers made their first aeroplane flight!

At various times, limits have been placed on practically every aspect of aircraft design and performance – only to be broken dramatically a few years later. The maximum possible speed for an aircraft was once thought to be about 240 km/h (150 mph) and in the 1920s a United States Navy committee decided that the largest possible aircraft would weigh about 20,000 kg (20 tons) – a Jumbo weighs 350,000 kg (345 tons). So the designers of aircraft have often proved the predictions wrong, but sometimes the designers have been wrong too. Their most common failing has been with large aircraft which were ahead of their time. Back in 1921 the Italian designer Count Gianni Caproni built a flying boat which had nine wings (three sets of three) and eight engines. It was intended to carry 100 passengers but after two short hops the project was abandoned. History repeated itself several times over

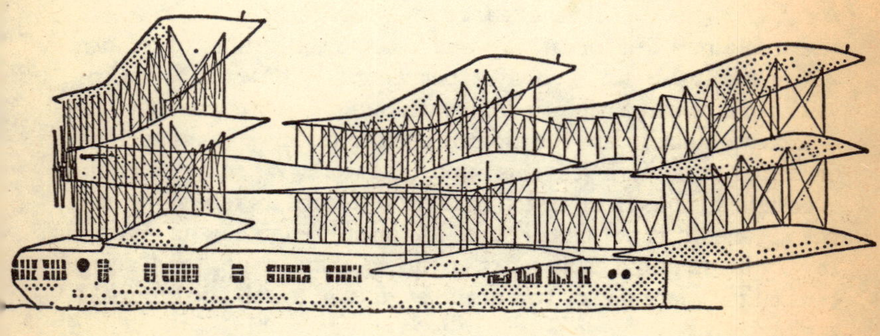

Caproni Ca 60 of 1921

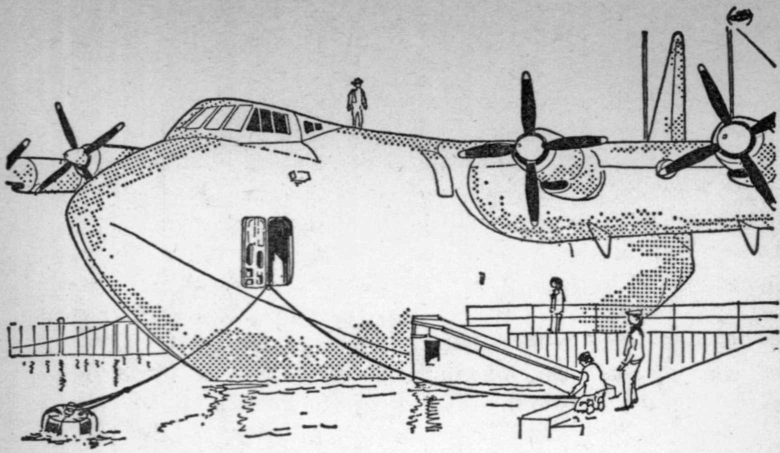

Hughes Hercules, 1947

and one of the most spectacular repeats was Howard Hughes' giant Hercules. This was also a flying boat with eight engines but it had only one wing, which had a span of 97.5 m (320 ft). The whole aircraft was made of wood and it was intended to carry 700 passengers. It made one flight in 1947 and never flew again.

To avoid making mistakes most aircraft designers carry out detailed research before embarking on a revolutionary project. For instance, the Concorde supersonic airliner was not built until the designers had tested out their ideas as thoroughly as possible. Concorde was designed to have a wing shaped like a paper dart or *slender delta* but this shape had to be tried out in the air so two research aircraft were built: the Handley Page HP 115 for low-speed trials and the BAC 221 for supersonic flight trials. The research aircraft of today may well become the airliner of tomorrow – if successful. If not, a costly experiment fails but it is better to fail with a research aircraft than with one full of passengers.

Less spectacular are the aircraft used to test new items such as engines, but nevertheless it is important work. When a new engine is designed it has to be tested in flight but until its reliability has been proved it is not usually used as the only engine in an aeroplane. It may be mounted as an extra engine, perhaps under the fuselage, or it may replace one or two of the engines of a well tried four-engined aircraft. These *flying test-beds* are often old aircraft which have served their time, so aircraft of the past are making a contribution to the future.

Whether airliners of the future will take-off vertically, travel in outer space or use some as yet undiscovered source of power is anyone's guess. For most passengers, hopes for the future are largely directed towards reliable, safe and cheap air travel.

Concorde and its research aircraft
1 Concorde   2 Handley Page HP 115 – slow speed trials with slender delta wing.   3 BAC 221 – supersonic trials with slender delta wing.
4 Avro Vulcan bomber – a flying test-bed carrying Concorde's Olympus engine under its fuselage.

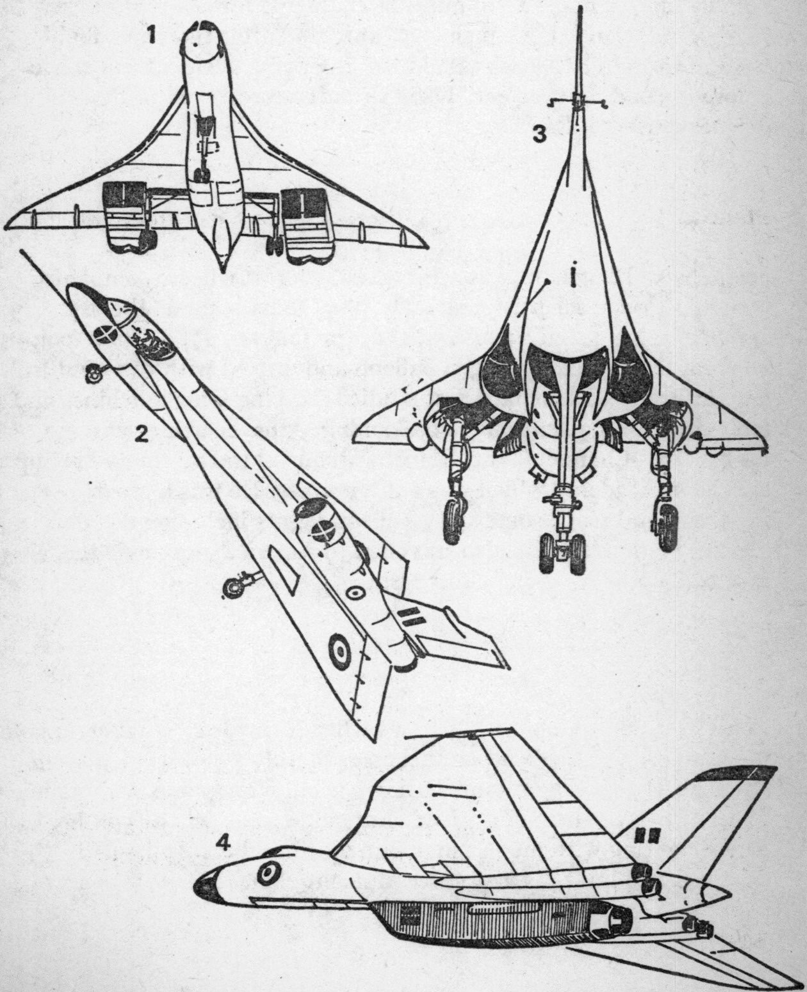

6 People

Alcock and Brown

Captain John Alcock and Lieutenant Arthur Whitten Brown made the first non-stop flight across the Atlantic Ocean in June 1919. They took off from Newfoundland in a converted Vickers Vimy bomber and 16 hours 12 minutes later they landed in a bog near Clifden in Ireland. Both men were knighted after their epic flight but unfortunately Alcock was killed in a flying accident in France before the end of the year. Their aircraft is preserved in the Science Museum, London.

Blanchard

Jean-Pierre Blanchard was a French balloonist who, accompanied by an American scientist called Dr John Jeffries, made the first aerial crossing of the English Channel in January 1785. They took off from Dover in a hydrogen balloon and drifted with the wind to land in France. Blanchard first studied flapping-wing machines and later turned his attentions to ballooning. After he achieved fame for his cross-Channel flight, Blanchard moved to Britain and set up a Balloon Academy which was not a success. He was a great showman and made some sixty balloon flights including one of 480 km (300 miles). He also travelled to America and made the first balloon flight in the United States.

Blériot

Louis Blériot became world famous when he made the first aeroplane flight across the English Channel on 25th July 1909. He flew from Calais to Dover in 37 minutes using a small monoplane he designed himself with the help of a friend, Raymond Saulnier. Blériot began experimenting with models in about 1900 and by 1907 he had designed and built his first successful aeroplane. Blériot was a pioneer of the monoplane, when most of the experts were following the Wright brothers' lead with clumsy biplanes. The cross-Channel flight resulted in Blériot receiving many orders for his monoplanes and several hundred were built between 1909 and 1914.

Cayley

Sir George Cayley was a prolific inventor of the early nineteenth century, often called the 'Father of Aeronautics'. In 1799 he sketched an aeroplane which had all the essentials to fly and a few years later he built the world's first model glider which was rather like a simple kite with the tail of a dart. Cayley carried out many experiments on different wing shapes using a whirling arm. In 1853 Cayley's coachman threatened to resign because he objected to flying his master's primitive full-size glider. Little is known about these flights, but a modern reconstruction of Cayley's glider has made some short hops. Cayley also produced ideas for a helicopter, an airship and the internal combustion engine.

Charles

Professor Jacques Charles was a scientist at the Paris Academy who became interested in the hot-air balloon experiments of the Montgolfier brothers. Professor Charles decided to try the new lightweight gas hydrogen in a balloon and his unmanned hydrogen balloon ascended on 27th August 1783. He was assisted by two brothers, Ainé and Cadet Robert, and on 1st December 1783 their first manned hydrogen balloon lifted off–carrying Professor Charles and one of the brothers on a 43-km (27-mile) flight. Unfortunately, the honour of making the world's first manned balloon flight had gone to a Montgolfier hot-air balloon just two weeks earlier.

Cobham

Sir Alan Cobham was a great pioneer of aviation in many different ways. He served in the Royal Flying Corps during the First World

War and started giving joy-rides in 1919. During the summer months of 1932–36 it has been estimated that almost a million people flew with his 'circuses'. Between 1924 and 1928 Cobham flew to Rangoon, Cape Town, Sydney and round Africa pioneering airline routes. He took part in several air races and campaigned for more aerodromes. In 1932 Cobham started experimenting with flight refuelling – transferring fuel from a tanker aircraft to a receiver in order to increase its range. His company, Flight Refuelling Limited, is still making refuelling systems for jet fighters.

Cockerell

Sir Christopher Cockerell invented the hovercraft in the 1950s. After experimenting with models and small boats Cockerell devised a vessel which was supported on a cushion of air. His main problem was to prevent this cushion of air, supplied by a large fan, from escaping around the edges of his hovercraft. At first he used a curtain of air but later he had to introduce a flexible rubber skirt. The first full-size hovercraft built to Cockerell's designs was the SR.N1 produced by Saunders-Roe in 1959. Today's hovercraft range from children's runabouts to cross-Channel ferries carrying sixty cars and 400 passengers.

Cody

Colonel Samuel Franklin Cody was a great pioneer of British aviation, yet he was an American ex-cowboy. His interest in aviation started with man-lifting kites and in 1905 his kites were bought by the British Government and Cody became a kite instructor. In 1907 he was assisting with the airship *Nulli Secundus* built at Farnborough and by 1908 he had designed and built his first aeroplane. On 16th October 1908 he made the first successful aeroplane flight in Britain, flying from Farnborough Common. In 1912 Cody won the first British Military Aeroplane competition but in August 1913 one of his aeroplanes crashed, killing Cody and his passenger.

Curtiss

Glenn H. Curtiss was an American pilot and aircraft designer whose main interest was marine aircraft. He started his career in aviation working for a team led by the famous inventor Alexander Graham Bell (who also invented the telephone). This team built four aeroplanes of which Curtiss designed the third called *June Bug*, and in 1908 Curtiss won a prize with *June Bug* for the first recorded flight of one kilometre in the USA. In 1909 Curtiss took his *Golden Flyer* to Rheims in France and won the Gordon Bennett trophy for the fastest aeroplane. The first aeroplane to take off from a ship was a Curtiss Model D (similar to *Golden Flyer*) in 1910 and in the following year Curtiss built a successful floatplane. Curtiss and his firm went on to produce many famous marine aircraft including the 1923 and 1925 Schneider Trophy winners.

Daimler and Benz

A powerful, lightweight engine was essential if a successful airship or an aeroplane was to be produced. However, the men who made the greatest contribution to the petrol engine as used in early aircraft were not thinking about an aero engine at all – they were developing an engine for road vehicles. In 1885 the German engineer Gottlieb Daimler, assisted by Wilhelm Maybach, built a working petrol engine and the following year their improved high-speed engine was fitted into a car. In the meantime another German engineer, Karl Benz, had also produced a working petrol engine. The Daimler Company changed its name to Mercedes and merged with Benz to produce cars, but the joint aero engine company became known as Daimler-Benz.

De Havilland

Sir Geoffrey de Havilland started experimenting with aircraft and engines of his own design in 1908. In the following year his first aircraft struggled into the air, and crashed. His second machine was more successful and de Havilland taught himself to fly. From

1910 to 1914 he acted as chief designer and test pilot at the Royal Aircraft Factory, Farnborough, where his most famous design was the B.E.2c biplane used by the RFC during the early years of the First World War. In 1914 de Havilland joined the Aircraft Manufacturing Co (Airco) and started producing the well-known D.H. series of aircraft. Then in 1920 the de Havilland Aircraft Company was founded and the famous Moth appeared in 1925. Many famous D.H. designs followed and Sir Geoffrey retained his interest in aviation until he died in 1965.

Fabre

Henri Fabre was a French scientist who specialised in the study of hydrodynamics (movement in water). His first seaplane, built in 1909, was not a success but in March the following year he built a second aircraft near Marseilles. Fabre's 'Hydravion' was a weird looking machine which flew tail-first with a pusher engine at the rear. It had three floats, one at the front and one under each wing. On 28th March 1910 Fabre was ready to test fly his floatplane – he had never flown before! At the second attempt he made a short hop and on the following day he made a flight of 6 km (3.75 miles). Fabre improved his Hydravion but decided that aviation was too expensive – although he continued to design floats for other people.

Fokker

Anthony Fokker was born in Java where his Dutch parents were living. He studied aeronautics in Germany where he built his first aeroplane with the aid of a friend and made his first 'hop'. Fokker rarely worked alone and 'his' designs were often the work of an employee who received little credit: nevertheless, Fokker was a great organiser and gifted pilot. He founded the Fokker Company near Berlin in 1912 and produced his monoplane Spin (Spider). When the War started in 1914 Fokker produced fighter aircraft for the Germans. In 1915 his E.1 monoplane created a sensation with its forward-firing machine gun. His Dr.1 triplane and D.VII biplane were also outstanding fighters. After the war, Fokker concentrated on airliners and his F.VII was widely used in the 1920s.

Handley Page

Sir Frederick Handley Page founded his company in 1909 and it survived until 1970. His first aeroplane, the Bluebird, was not a success but in 1910 he demonstrated an improved version nicknamed the 'Yellow Peril'. But 'HP' was not a great pilot: he concentrated on the design and manufacture of his aeroplanes. During the First World War he specialised in the design of heavy bombers such as the V/1500 which was intended for raids on Berlin. The company operated an airline after the war and HP turned his attention to making aeroplanes safer by fitting slats to their wings. His large airliner, the H.P.42, was fitted with slats and had one of the best safety records of all time.

Hargrave

Lawrence Hargrave was born in London but emigrated to Australia at the age of seventeen. From about 1884 he started experimenting with flapping wing aircraft and then went on to lightweight engines. His most important aeronautical work was the development and perfection of the box-kite during the 1890s. Hargrave's ideas were adapted for children's kites and man-lifting kites but they had an even wider influence. Because the box-kite was very stable in the air, its basic shape was used by several early aeroplane designers such as Alberto Santos-Dumont and the French Voisin brothers.

Hawker

Harry G. Hawker was an Australian who came to Britain in 1911 and soon joined T. O. M. Sopwith as a mechanic. He learned to fly in 1912 and during the First World War he became an outstanding test pilot with the Sopwith Aviation Company. In 1919 he attempted to fly the Atlantic in a Sopwith Atlantic biplane, with Lieutenant Commander K. K. Mackenzie-Grieve as navigator. They crashed into the sea but were rescued. In 1920 the Sopwith company closed down and a new one was formed with the name H. G. Hawker Engineering Company. Harry Hawker was a director but unfortunately he was killed while testing the aircraft he was to fly in the Aerial Derby of 1921. The Hawker company suffered a severe loss but went on to become one of Britain's most successful aircraft companies.

Heinkel

Professor Ernst Heinkel's first experience of aviation was probably the sight of a Zeppelin being destroyed by fire after it had been struck by lightning. That was in 1908 when he was an engineering student and just three years later Heinkel had designed and built his first aeroplane. His main interest throughout his life was high speed aeroplanes and by 1922 he had founded his own company. In 1935 Heinkel met Wernher von Braun, the German rocket expert, and they produced the He 176 rocket-powered aeroplane which flew in June 1939 and later reached 805 km/h (500 mph). In 1936 Heinkel engaged an engineer called Pabst von Ohain who was working on gas turbine engines and this partnership resulted in the world's first jet aircraft. The diminutive He 178 first flew in August 1939 but unfortunately for Heinkel, Hitler would not order any rocket or jet aircraft.

Johnson

Amy Johnson was working as a secretary when she decided to fly in her spare time. She joined the London Aeroplane Club and by June 1929 she had qualified for her pilot's licence. Then she went on to qualify as a mechanic and bought her own aeroplane – a secondhand de Havilland Moth which she called *Jason*. On 5th May 1930 she set out on a solo flight to Australia and 19½ days later she reached Port Darwin: she had not broken the record but she had become the first woman to fly solo to Australia and this made her a world-famous figure. In 1932 Amy married Jim

Mollison, another record-breaking pilot, and together they broke many records. Amy was killed in 1941 while ferrying a military aircraft: she parachuted into the sea but was drowned.

Leonardo da Vinci

Leonardo was born in the village of Vinci in Italy in 1452, but later moved to Milan where he painted *The Last Supper*. He was an outstanding painter, sculptor, mathematician, architect and engineer. Most of his inventions were just sketches of ideas for he rarely built his ingenious machines. He drew detailed plans for a man-powered flapping-wing machine after studying birds and bats. Leonardo also sketched a helicopter and a parachute which was shaped like a pyramid. Although Leonardo intended to publish these inventions he never did so, and they remained undiscovered until the nineteenth century – by which time other inventors had also had similar ideas.

Lilienthal

Otto Lilienthal, a German engineer, was one of the most important names in the history of the aeroplane for he was the first man to fly with wings. As a boy, Otto and his brother Gustav fitted wings to their arms and tried in vain to fly. Otto became a successful engineer but he never lost his interest in flying and studied the flight of birds in great detail. By 1891 he was able to make short gliding flights in his monoplane hang-glider. Lilienthal built many gliders, including several biplanes, and he was able to make controlled flights of about 350 m (1150 ft). By 1896 he had made over 2000 flights but unfortunately in August of that year he crashed and died of his injuries.

Lindbergh

Charles Lindbergh was an airmail pilot in the United States during the 1920s. He was a gifted pilot and an above average navigator, so the prize of $25,000 being offered for the first flight between New York and Paris attracted his attention. Lindbergh decided to fly solo and use a specially-built Ryan monoplane which had only one engine – decisions which worried his friends. However, he took off on 20th May 1927 and 33 hours 39 minutes later he landed in Paris to a hero's welcome. This flight captured the imagination of America and gave aviation a great boost. Unfortunately, Lindbergh was in the news again in 1932 when his son was kidnapped and killed. The following year Lindbergh and his wife Anne started a series of flights surveying possible routes for airline services on behalf of Pan American Airways.

Montgolfier brothers

Etienne and Joseph Montgolfier were paper-makers of Annonay near Lyons in France. From simple experiments with a fire, in which light objects were carried up the chimney, the brothers went on to produce a silk bag which they filled with hot air and which then rose up into the air. A larger balloon made from linen and lined with paper was demonstrated to the public in the marketplace at Annonay. Then followed a balloon to carry the first living passengers into the air – a sheep, a cock and a duck. By October 1783 the Montgolfiers had built a hot-air balloon which could lift a man, and tethered tests were carried out. Then on 21st November 1783 Pilâtre de Rozier and the Marquis d'Arlandes made the first ever aerial voyage. Ascending in hot-air balloons (or Montgolfières as they were called) became a popular sport.

Pilcher

Percy Pilcher was a marine engineer who became a lecturer at Glasgow University. In 1895 he built his first glider, the Bat, but before flying it he visited Germany to consult Otto Lilienthal, who had already made many gliding flights. Pilcher returned and flew his hang-gliders on the north bank of the River Clyde. He moved to Kent and built his most successful glider, the Hawk, in 1896. Pilcher was eager to build a powered aeroplane and he had plans to fly a powered version of the Hawk and a powered triplane. With his partner Walter G. Wilson he designed and built a new aero engine which was tested in August 1899, but unfortunately Pilcher crashed while flying the Hawk glider on 30th September and died two days later.

Santos-Dumont

Alberto Santos-Dumont was a Brazilian who lived in Paris. He built his first airship in 1898 and went on to build a series of airships which improved as the irrepressible Santos-Dumont learned from his mistakes. He made several attempts to win a large prize for the first flight around the Eiffel Tower: on 19th October 1901 he succeeded with Airship No 6. Santos-Dumont went on to build eight more airships and then, in 1906, turned his attention to aeroplanes. His first aeroplane was called 14-bis because it was tested slung underneath Airship No 14. This tail-first machine was based on Hargrave's box-kite design and made the first aeroplane flight in Europe. Santos-Dumont's most successful aeroplane was the tiny 'Demoiselle' (or Dragonfly) which was widely used by sporting pilots.

Sikorsky

Igor Ivan Sikorsky was a remarkable man, for three times he started from the beginning and built up a world-famous operation. He was brought up in Russia where he started building helicopters in 1910, but he soon turned his attention to aeroplanes. By 1913 he had designed and flown the world's first four-engined aircraft which was far larger than other aircraft at that time. In 1919 Sikorsky emigrated to the United States and started a new company. Sikorsky flying boats became very successful in the 1920s and 1930s and were used extensively by Pan American Airways. The company was taken over and Igor Sikorsky started a new career as a helicopter designer. His VS-300 flew in 1939 and within a few years Sikorsky helicopters were leading the world.

Sopwith

Thomas Sopwith enjoyed dabbling with motorcycles as a schoolboy and progressed to motorcars, speedboats and balloons. He bought an aeroplane and learned to fly in 1910 – at the age of twenty-two. Within a few days of obtaining his pilot's certificate, Sopwith set up a British duration record of 3 hours 12 minutes and went on to win many prizes including the Aerial Derby of 1912. During the First World War, the newly formed Sopwith Aviation Company produced some of Britain's best fighters, such as the Pup, Camel, 1½ Strutter and Snipe. In 1920 the Sopwith Company closed down and a new company was founded called H. G. Hawker Engineering Company with T. O. M. Sopwith as one of the directors. He resigned as Chairman of the huge Hawker Siddeley Group in 1963.

von Braun

Baron Wernher von Braun was a very talented young man and his father was a Minister in the German Government. Wernher was interested in rockets at the age of eighteen and joined a group of rocket enthusiasts. He qualified as an engineer in 1932 and learned to fly soon afterwards. In 1937 Dr von Braun was made technical director of the Germans' secret rocket establishment. Here the A4 (or V-2 as it was known in Britain) rocket missile was developed under von Braun's guidance. When the Second World War ended von Braun went to the United States where he continued his work on large space rockets including the Apollo-Saturn V which landed men on the moon in 1969. His next project was the re-usable space shuttle.

Wallis

Barnes Wallis started his aviation career in 1913 when he joined Vickers Limited as an airship designer working on the rigid airship No 9. In 1924 he became Chief Engineer of the Airship Guarantee Company which built the successful airship R100. Unfortunately, the rival R101 crashed and it was decided to scrap the R100. Wallis had developed a latticework (or geodetic) structure for airships and he adapted it for aircraft when he joined Vickers Aviation Limited in 1934. The Wellesley and Wellington bombers were extremely robust thanks to their geodetic construction. Wallis turned his attention to bombs and designed large penetration bombs and the famous dam-busting bouncing bombs. Then he worked on swing-wing supersonic aircraft but his ideas were never fully developed.

Whittle

Frank Whittle served in the RAF as an apprentice and became a flying instructor. He patented a jet engine in 1930 and a few years later he convinced the authorities that his ideas would work. He was allowed to study and carry out research at Cambridge University. A company called Power Jets was set up and by 1937 they had built one of Whittle's engines and run it in a ground test bed. Whittle had a hard fight to obtain support but eventually they were allowed to build a jet aeroplane: the Gloster E28/39 made its maiden flight in May 1941, by which time the German Heinkel He 178 jet aeroplane had flown. However, Whittle's engine was improved and powered many aircraft whereas the Heinkel's engine did not.

Wright brothers

Wilbur and Orville Wright were in the bicycle business in Dayton, Ohio and in the 1890s they became interested in flying. They studied the exploits of Otto Lilienthal and the other gliding pioneers and then set about solving some of the unsolved problems in their own way. First they developed a means of controlling a glider with movable control surfaces – instead of weight shifting. Then they designed and built their own lightweight engine and on 17th December 1903 they made the world's first aeroplane flight in their biplane *Flyer*. Much of their flying was done secretly – and so when Wilbur demonstrated their Model A in France during 1908 the European pioneers were amazed at its performance.

Zeppelin

Count Ferdinand von Zeppelin was founder of the German Zeppelin company and originator of the huge rigid airships which were named after him. The first one was built in 1900 and was only partially successful, but improved Zeppelins were soon carrying passengers between German cities. These services ended in 1914, by which time von Zeppelin was already designing airships for military purposes. During the First World War Zeppelins were used to patrol the seas in search of enemy warships and drop bombs on targets in Britain. Just before he died in 1917, at the age of seventy-eight, von Zeppelin had turned his attention from airships to large aeroplanes.

30387 X